The Caring Classroom

**A Guide for Teachers Troubled
by the Difficult Student and
Classroom Disruption**

Dewey J. Carducci and Judith B. Carducci

Bull Publishing Company

Copyright 1984
Dewey J. Carducci, and
Judith B. Carducci

Bull Publishing Co.
P.O. Box 208
Palo Alto, CA 94302

ISBN
  Cloth: 0-915950-61-8
  Paper: 0-915950-62-6

Library of Congress Catalog
Card Number: 84-70277

Distributed in the United States by
  Kampmann & Company, Inc.
  9 East 40th Street
  New York, NY 10016

Design: Michelle Taverniti
Cover illustration: Julie Peterson

To our son, David, with love.

"*The Caring Classroom* is an extremely well written, easily understood, and practically applicable book for any classroom teacher.

"I especially like the advice to break the class into triads. I have often talked about dealing with a class in small groups, because students would cooperate better, but it has never been spelled out as clearly as it is in this book, where the authors explain how triads might help a teacher to really bring a class under control.

"I see applications in this book for every classroom situation."

William Glasser, M.D.
Author, *Reality Therapy, Schools Without Failure,* and *The Pictures in Your Head* (fall, 1984).

This is a teacher-to-teacher book. It has been written by wise teachers who are veterans of work with troubled youth.

Though it draws primarily on one teacher's experience, its applications are very broad. It provides a realistic, workable model for a way to transform volatile, rebellious youth into responsible students. Many teachers are desperately searching for an alternative to the power struggles that so often contaminate their teaching; Dewey Carducci provides such an alternative.

This easily-read book gives one the feeling of spending a few evenings as a guest in the living room of a master teacher, one who draws on learning theory only as a means to an end. This is not a research-oriented book, and the authors acknowledge that they borrow freely from a range of sources; but the work has its own originality nevertheless, as it harmonizes various strategies to create the synergy of a caring classroom.

After a brief look at the standard classifications of behavioral disorders, Carducci quickly leaves behind the structure of DSM III (Diagnostic Statistical Manual of the American Psychiatric Association). He focuses on how people with behavior disorders frequently relate to each other, and he utilizes the prison milieu concept of the "sliding partner." This is the irresponsible student who manipulates others for his own private benefit, leaving a trail of frustration and turmoil. He becomes one of the prime targets for change, in the Carducci process of creating an attitude of caring in order to create an atmosphere for learning.

With such students, how does one establish initial control, without becoming a cop? The key is to create a class climate of committed, positive peer influence. From the start the teacher models concern, but at the same time s/he must assert controls designed to secure student commitment. Rejecting elaborate behavior modification schemes or the use of punishment, Dewey establishes a three-tiered system of tools for gaining control even where the starting point is chaos, in the period before the caring classroom can begin to function. Procedures are described for use of 1) a classroom "time out" area, 2) an out-of-the-classroom "holding area," and 3) a "last resort conference," which rallies the support of all the responsible adults who can help the student get control of himself.

The goal is to phase out these teacher-directed controls, as students are taught to assume self and peer responsibility.

Perhaps the most ingenious contribution of Dewey is the use of *triads,* subgroups of three students, as the heart of his behavioral control and affective education system. We learn how these triads are formed, how they multiply the teacher's effectiveness through peer tutorial instruction, and how the teacher's influence (and security) is expanded—while simultaneously the ability of any individual troublemaker to exert negative influence is curtailed. As students assume greater responsibility, the chaotic classroom becomes relaxed and productive, a wonder to those who saw these same students regularly destroy the learning environment in their earlier classrooms.

At a time when it is easy to give up, when many believe that nothing can work with disruptive students, Dewey shows how a teacher can in fact create a potent caring classroom, one which draws the best from young people. Before reading this, a teacher might well believe that working with such youth leaves only two options: either to wield the intimidating control of a drill sergeant, or to give in and be controlled by them. Dewey describes a truly viable third option, which can emancipate the teacher from these no-win choices, and allow him to really pursue his profession of teaching.

Larry Brendtro, Ph.D.
Author, *The Other 23 Hours, Positive Peer Culture,* and *Re-educating Troubled Youth*

Acknowledgements

We want to express our gratitude to the following:

Frank Longo, and John and Annie Romanyshyn for professional inspiration;

Claire Fitzpatrick, Phyllis Estis, Deborah Allen, Johnnie Henderson, Gordon and Selene Loomis, Chris Heim, Ronald Kingsley, Gene Kleindienst, and Eli Bower for critical suggestions and encouragement, and Bill Wilson for his help as a consultant;

James Greene, for permitting the development of the model during his tenure as administrator of Harry L. Eastman School;

Tony Vivino and Hal Estis for moral support when it counted;

Joseph Carducci, for professional consultation;

Dave Bull, for believing in The Caring Classroom, and for having the wisdom, humor, and good taste that made the editing process a pleasure.

Table of Contents

Introduction

Ours is an aggressive culture, a distraught culture. Schools can no longer fulfill their total obligation by teaching the three R's to normal and disturbed pupils . . . [We are] *being literally swamped by pupils who demonstrate the culture's arrested affective teaching . . . The pressing dilemmas which bring us to our knees are matters of feelings, attitudes, and values—the emotional components of living. These determine how we feel about ourselves, what our motivations are, and how we treat those about us. The weave of school experiences should be comprised of the warp of thinking and the woof of feeling.*

William C. Morse*

*William C. Morse, *Classroom Disturbance: The Principal's Dilemma* (Arlington, Virginia: The Council for Exceptional Children, 1971), pp. viii–ix.

W *hy a Caring Classroom?*

This is a "how-to" book—a survival kit for teachers of emotionally disturbed, disruptive students. The tools, ideas, suggestions, and philosophy presented here have all been classroom-tested over many years by the author, borrowing freely from whatever sources seemed to offer relief and hope, changing and adding and expanding and integrating as new applications suggested themselves. Although the process has been eclectic and pragmatic, it has been so within definite limits; it is not a simple matter of the ends justifying whatever works. There are certain important principles which provide the foundation for the practices set forth here, which bind them all together.

Any one of the students in my classroom in an institution for court-committed delinquents could easily disrupt an entire class of "normal" learners. Yet visitors to my class are struck by the relaxation of both students and teacher, the orderliness in which education is taking place, and the kindness and mutual respect with which interpersonal transactions are conducted. It is a "caring" classroom.

There is no magic in establishing a caring classroom: there is a basic philosophy which underlies it, and specific tools and procedures which are used to build it. This book spells out the philosophy, knowledge, skills, and procedures that work.

Since the certification of teachers in Special Education, and the passage of P. L. 94-142, more attention has been focused on the needs of children with behavior disorders, and more programs to meet those needs have been started. Yet the teachers and their administrators often feel as though they are re-inventing the wheel. Neither schools of education nor in-service training fully equip teachers for the enormous stress and the seemingly endless variety of challenges with which these students can bombard them.

For example, at a faculty meeting, a staff were asked to list the topics most crucial for in-service training. The list is poignant, redolent of stress:

How is a teacher supposed to teach a class which is out of control or has a student out of control?

How do you formulate strategies to work with these children?

What do we do when the kids walk out of the Holding Room? How can we be sure they reach the Holding Room when sent there?

What is a teacher supposed to do when a student will not accept his authority and then refuses to leave the room?

What can be done to make the administration meet *their* responsibilities?

We need a program for dealing with disruptive students in this school.

What are concrete ways of dealing with behavior problems?

What is going on in the minds of disruptive students?

What abnormalities are "normal" with our students [seriously behaviorally disordered]?

How do you teach behavior skills?

The people who posed these questions are experienced teachers. They are also in pain. They face the events which give rise to these questions day after day after day. They deserve help.

The purpose of this book is to give help with exactly this kind of question. Trial and error is a long, inefficient, and frustrating way to learn to cope with these challenges, and is often very costly, in disillusionment and "teacher burn-out." Further, what appears to "work" in the short run, if viewed only from functional or pragmatic criteria, and not evaluated from the perspective of an overall philosophy and value system, may in reality be undermining or preventing your ultimate goal. Today's "success" may be the root of tomorrow's failure.

Why a "caring" classroom? Why not a quiet one? Or a "fun" one? The question is crucial to the entire question of "why educate?"—about which volumes have been written, and which requires facing the issue of what are the essential qualities of healthy, mature human beings.

More will be said of these considerations in the body of this book, but perhaps it will suffice to say here that the healthy, mature person is able to give and receive love, to care about himself and others, and, in turn, to inspire their caring about him.* Emanating from this prime characteristic are others, such as the ability to make wise decisions, that will result in the well-being of self and others and that respect the rights of self and others, the ability to set and work towards goals, the ability to solve prob-

---

*See William Glasser, *Reality Therapy: A New Approach to Psychiatry* (NY: Harper & Row, 1965)

4

lems, and the ability to take responsibility and be accountable for one's behavior.

The "caring" classroom is based on the belief that it is the business of education to support and assist the growth of the student toward maturity—that is, toward the fulfilling of personality in the ability to love and be loved, with all that that implies. Conversely, it is based on the belief that education is not merely the imparting of knowledge, the training in a skill, or the conditioning of one person by another to do what the person in authority prescribes.*

Some teachers conduct their classrooms as if the goal of education were training in obedience and submission, or training in getting the right answer on the test, or training in how to make even the most odious tasks in life "fun." There is nothing at all wrong with knowledge, obedience, submission, knowing the right answer on a test, or having fun; they are, however, by-products rather than goals of education. When the by-product is mistaken for the goal, education begins to wither.

"Caring" is not something that "comes naturally."** A child whose basic needs have been more frustrated than fulfilled will become increasingly un-

---

*For an excellent presentation expanding on the definition, philosophy, and goals of education, see "Schooling—Only a Part of Education," pp. 9–12 of *The Paideia Proposal, An Educational Manifesto*, by Mortimer J. Adler (N.Y.: MacMillan, 1980).

**The following presentation on child development is the authors' distillation of the literature, as represented by the bibliography at the end of the chapter, tempered of course by our own professional beliefs and values.

able to care about himself or others. The extreme result of being deprived of love was described years ago by John Bowlby in his studies of "hospitalism." Infants deprived of consistent mothering (even though given good physical care in hospitals) did not learn to talk and walk normally, and some even died.

Children whose basic needs for food, clothing, shelter, love, new experience, sleep, or security are more often frustrated than met will become depressed, clogged up with guilt, anger, grief, and anxiety—the painful feelings that result from unmet needs. These feelings, though painful, are legitimate and realistic—Mother Nature's way of sending the signal that things are drastically wrong.* The child's way of dealing with this signal and these feelings is what causes difficulty for him or for his society, including his teacher.

One child will keep the feelings inside where they are most painful only to him. Suffering internally, he may appear compliant, passive, sad, wan, or withdrawn—but not a source of pain to others, and therefore easily overlooked. Another child will act the feelings out—especially the anger which he substitutes for the even more painful feeling of sadness or grief—and thereby get attention, because his behavior now brings pain to others. The attention may

---

*For a discussion of the positive role of pain, see the chapter entitled "Suffering" in Allen Wheelis, *How People Change*, (New York: Harper & Row, 1973). Also see Norman Cousins, *Anatomy of An Illness*.

not be the kind that satisfies his original need, however; since anger begets more anger, and aggression provokes counter-aggression, he often finds that, far from getting his needs met, he is only compounding his problem.

However, immediate indulgence of every need does not automatically produce a caring person. The child whose every need is immediately met, who is loved unconditionally with no expectation of love in return, will more often than not grow into a self-centered "spoiled" person who believes that all good things are his right, regardless of the rights and feelings of others. Caring is not learned by example alone, nor by being loved, alone. Caring must be taught, and caring behavior expected and elicited. Moreover, since life in the real world is not a process of immediate gratification of all desires, there will always be some frustration, and as a result some painful feelings. How to deal with painful feelings must be taught also.

It is of utmost importance that the teacher understand and respect the painful feelings which students bring with them into the classroom. It is the painful feelings of guilt, anger, grief, and anxiety, resulting from unmet needs, that are the impetus for the behavior which disrupts the classrooms, creates chaos in schools, brings education to a standstill, and drives teachers from the profession. These feelings are normal and natural, a normal functioning of the human organism. They are not "bad"—only painful, only *there*. However, what the child *does* about the feelings may be very bad—for himself or for others.

Feelings do not go away because they are inconvenient or painful. Many teachers expect that the child will leave his feelings at the threshold of the classroom. He can't. It's impossible. The child cannot split himself off from his feelings: he is all of one piece. What he thinks is inextricably bound up with what he feels.

He has choices about what he thinks and does, but he doesn't know that until somebody teaches him.* Through trial and error he may have discovered one way of dealing with his feelings, which he favors. If he is lucky, his way will be appropriate and satisfying; in the case of most disturbed children, however, because of their immaturity, and the paucity of good examples and the potency of bad examples, their way will not be appropriate and satisfying, and will lead only to more trouble.

What the teacher does is crucial. The teacher can punish the child's behavior directly, or reject the child and the behavior—which will result either in suppression with no growth, and with greater pain and danger for the child, or else will result in more intense acting-out. Or the teacher can accept the child, with his feelings, as a person in pain and in need of help, and teach the child how to deal with his feelings in acceptable ways that will result in fulfillment of his needs, and therefore in less pain and less need to act in self-defeating ways.

To teach a child how to behave in ways that are need-fulfilling is, by definition, to teach him how to

---

*See Chapter V, below, on Classic Problem-Solving.

care about himself and others. The person who *cares about* himself and others is able to *take care* of himself—to get his needs met—and to respect himself because others respect him and because he is potent and adequate.

The child who cares about himself and others is no longer so bombarded by painful feelings that he needs all his energy to deal with them; he is free to use his energy for intellectual pursuits. After having been in a caring classroom for a few weeks, students begin to exhibit a serenity that amazes the adults who have known them in the past. With this calmness comes a sudden ability to learn: they begin to "take off" academically—to learn quickly and easily math and language skills that had completely eluded them during years of previous schooling.

The teacher who is able to teach caring is in our opinion giving his students the single most important gift that one person can give another. And the teacher is in an ideal situation to do this, because of the length, intensity, and consistency of the time he spends with the students, and the potency of his influence. How to teach caring in the classroom situation, as an integral part of the whole educational process, is the subject of this book.

Although the problems addressed here are found in greater numbers in "special" classrooms, they can be found (in more isolation but not necessarily with less intensity) in any "regular" classroom. The approach given here is applicable in any setting, in any classroom, with any students, because it addresses the needs of all students to be taught to cope, to grow, and care, and be cared about. Thus, any teacher will find these concepts useful and adaptable to his situation.

On the Use of Tools

In the following pages, a number of tools are described, along with circumstances under which each is useful, and instructions for using them. A tool is only as good as the skill with which it is used and the appropriateness of the circumstances under which it is used. An ax is an excellent tool, as is a hammer or a scalpel. But in the hands of an amateur, the ax can cut off a foot; and it is not useful, even in the hands of a skilled woodsman, in a delicate surgical procedure. The proper use of tools requires long practice and good judgment. Without practice and judgment they may be useless at best, harmful at worst.

A good tool used for the wrong reasons, and the wrong motives, may be harmful—an ax can be used as a murder weapon. For example: Much is said in the following pages about tools for gaining control. I have seen these tools used skillfully to obtain control in classrooms, but in some of these situations the motives for gaining control were bad, and as a result the control was harmful to the students' ultimate growth.

Control can be punishing and stunting rather than growth-enhancing; it can be used to belittle or to lord it over someone, or to produce unthinking followers with no judgment of their own, perpetually dependent on an authority figure to tell them what to do. Again, control skillfully obtained but for the wrong motives can be destructive.

If a tool is used in a clumsy way, for the wrong reasons, or in inappropriate circumstances, the tool is not to blame. The tool is no less a tool and its usefulness is in no way diminished. I have seen teachers angrily declare that a tool "doesn't work," when the real problem was that the tool was being used improperly or for the wrong reasons. Some teachers want instant results from a tool they have not yet learned to use, with students whose problems developed over many years. All the tools given here are good tools, but the user may need willingness and patience to put in the hours of practice needed to perfect the skill to use them properly.

The biggest problem for teachers in using these tools, in addition to the feeling of urgent need for instant results, is the danger of closed-mindedness as to their place in the educational process. Teachers can become doctrinaire, and insist that the tool fit their preconceived goals—somewhat like using a scalpel to cut down a tree, and then becoming disillusioned with scalpels and with anyone who says a scalpel is useful.

Some teachers, acutely and chronically suffering from classroom disruption, and finding that nothing they have been doing is effective, will denounce with heat a tool that could be effective for them, if only they would be open-minded about their goals. If they can't have success on their own terms, they don't want success. They would rather the patient die than that they, the teacher, should change.

Change. Change is what teachers want—but often only for their students. They want their students' behavior to change (and rightly so), but some may strenuously resist changing their own philosophy or approach in order to make it possible for students to change. They agree that change is fine, so long as it's for the other person. And yet, when all is said and done, the only person we can change is ourselves.

The teacher cannot force the students to change, but he can change the way he himself interacts with the students, and even can change the reasons he interacts with them; he may, thereby, assist the students to do their own changing.

Likewise, this book cannot change anybody. If you as a teacher, are not satisfied with the way you are dealing with classroom disruption, if you are finding that your approach is not working and are looking for something that will work, if you are willing to change some of your outlook if that would help you, and are willing to invest your time and effort for ultimate success, without insisting on "instant cures," you will find this book helpful. On the other hand, if you want the tools to do the work for you, and the students to change without your being willing to change first, then read no further. This book is not for you.

Change is hard and slow and doesn't follow a smooth pattern. People do not grow in steady consistent ways. They have growth spurts and plateaus, and, frequently, setbacks. My own classroom is not always relaxed and orderly, although caring is the norm and disruption is the exception. Sometimes, when a new student who doesn't know how to care joins us, or when a student whose caring is still very fragile and tentative breaks down under some inevitable stress, explosive behavior will occur.

That is not a time for despair, but rather a time to tell oneself that one really knows what he knows, that life is predictably unpredictable, that students (and we ourselves) grow in zigzags rather than straight lines, and that now is the time to use one's tools rather than discard them. But sometimes a new tool is needed, and then a skilled toolmaker, who understands the problem and the circumstances of use, is needed.

Tools should never be designed without thorough research and knowledge. I have seen teachers who had no understanding of the dynamics of disturbed children, who had discarded proven tools as "useless" because they didn't produce the immediate results they wanted, sit down together with the intention of inventing a brand new tool. But they didn't understand their "clients," didn't understand health or illness, or the healing process, or their own role in the process. They were engaging in a sharing of ignorance, which would waste time at best, and produce a dangerous tool at worst.

Some people believe that "common sense" and "instinct" are all that are needed to teach disturbed children. By "common sense," and "instinct," however, they do not mean the good judgment that is born of long experience and educated understanding. Rather, they seem to mean "whatever feels good or comfortable."

In this existential world, people often confuse "what feels good" with "what is right." The two are not necessarily the same at all. "What feels good" ("common sense" or "instinct") can vary unpredictably from one person to another, and even within the same person over a period of time, and may have little or nothing to do with the needs of the student or the situation. One teacher's "instinct" or "common sense" may be to "paddle the kid" (for his own good, of course), while another's may be to pamper him and keep him from suffering any consequences of his behavior; still a third's may be to ignore him in the hope that he (or his behavior) will go away, and that of a fourth teacher may be refuse to have him in class altogether.

This "instinct" relates to the needs of the reactor rather than to the needs of the student, and is inconsistent, often depending more on mood or state of digestion than on any well-grounded concept of what is needed and appropriate. The teacher who feels like "paddling the kid" today may feel like humoring him tomorrow, depending on whether that teacher, who had a fight with his wife today, makes up with her tonight. That is a very unprofessional basis for acting. Yet "common sense" and "instinct" are treasured by some teachers faced with teaching disturbed students.

Perhaps this affection for "common sense" and "instinct" is really an attempt to relegate an overwhelmingly stressful problem to a manageable level, by minimizing it as "an ordinary routine little problem which anybody should know how to cope with." In any case, it isn't working. If "common sense" and "instinct" were sufficient to the task, why are so many teachers still so desperately unhappy about the way their disturbed students continue to behave, and so despairing of the adequacy of their own methods for coping with these students?

The same can be said of "opinion" as of "common sense" and "instinct." There are right ways and wrong ways, helpful ways and harmful ways and useless ways, to deal with these same problems. Subjective "opinion" is of no help at all.

Educators need to stop minimizing the problem and approaching it haphazardly. It is a big problem and they have every right to be frustrated and in pain. The need therefore is to respect the problem more and "common sense" and "opinion" less. Knowing what one *doesn't* know is as important as knowing what one does know. It does not lead to loss of self-respect, but rather to courage, realistic humility, the skillful use of consultation, and ultimately a satisfying solution to the problem.

There is always more to be learned—from "experts," from peers, and from our students themselves. With learning comes good judgment—educated judgment, in which the professional uses himself, including his knowledge and his instincts, in a controlled way for the benefit of the students. His empathy, intuition, "instinct," "opinions," and "common sense" are now all of a piece, carefully harnessed and directed.

It is our hope that this book will not only provide a useful step along this continuum, but will stimulate still further and better discoveries. It is also our hope that this learning process will be exciting, and will reward you with a satisfying professional career, rather than the devastating alienation and exhaustion that is driving teachers from the field and making armed camps out of schools.

Note to Reader: *Although we have included in this book a few suggested exercizes and work sheets (example: exercizes on dealing with Rescuer-Persecutor-Victim triangles and Data-Assessment-Treatment Planning), we have generally avoided making this into a programmed learning workbook. The reason for this is because of the importance we place on the professional creativity of the teacher* and *the value we place on the coaching-supervising-peer support role. This book cannot substitute for either of these.*

While we want to be clear about our philosophy and methods, and hope that the material in this book will be practical and usable, it is not meant to be used all alone. There are many books which give collections of worksheets and exercizes that can be adapted to the Caring Classroom, and we have included some in the bibliographies at the ends of appropriate chapters. Use your own uniqueness and your own creativity, and get help from your peers and administrators.

Suggested Readings

Aichhorn, August. *Wayward Youth*. New York: The Viking Press, 1935.

Bettelheim, Bruno. *Love Is Not Enough*. Glencoe, Ill.: The Free Press, 1950.
About the treatment of emotionally disturbed children at the University of Chicago's Sonia Shankman Orthogenic School.

————. *Truants From Life, The Rehabilitation of Emotionally Disturbed Children*. Glencoe, Ill.: The Free Press, 1955. Cases from the Sonia Shankman Orthogenic School.

Bowlby, John. *Child Care And the Growth of Love* (2nd Edition). New York: Penguin Books, 1965.

Dennison, George. *The Lives of Children*. New York: Random House, 1969.

Fantini, Mario. "Disciplined Caring," *The Phi Delta Kappan,* Nov., 1980, pp. 182–184.

Fraiberg, Selma. *The Magic Years*. New York: Charles Scribners' Sons, 1959.

Freud, Anna. *The Ego and the Mechanisms of Defense*. New York: International Universities Press, 1946.

Montagu, M. F. Ashley. *The Direction of Human Development*. New York: Harper and Brothers, 1955.

Redl, Fritz. *When We Deal With Children*. New York: The Free Press, 1966.

Rothman, Esther P. *Troubled Teachers*. New York: David McKay, 1977.

Trieschman, Albert E., et. al. *The Other 23 Hours*. Chicago: Aldine, 1969.
A basic book on child-care work with emotionally disturbed children in a therapeutic milieu, helpful reading for teachers of students in an institutional setting.

1. Who are the Problem Students?

*The business of a school is not or should not be
mere instruction but the life of the child.*
                              George Dennison
                              The Lives of Children

What are the students with behavior disorders
like? How do they behave? In the Introduction, we discussed the two major dynamics behind
their behavior: (1) painful feelings, arising from frustration of fulfillment of basic needs, clamoring for
expression; and (2) severe poverty of appropriate
behavioral repertoire to express these feelings.
When it comes to adequate behavior, most of these
youngsters are destitute. The destitution can be seen
in the severe limitation and lack of variety in the
behavior choices they favor.

Generally, each child's behavior is typical of only one of five behavioral adaptation categories,* the first four of which will be discussed here. (We will not deal with the psychoses here. Childhood schizophrenia, and autism, which may be either a psychosis or a severe retardation, are too special for the scope of this book.) Simply stated, these categories are:

a. Aggression
b. Passivity
c. Passive-aggressiveness
d. Transient aggressiveness or passivity in an otherwise normal personality
e. Psychosis

---

*The reader interested in detailed description and classification of these behavior categories is referred to the *Diagnostic and Statistical Manual of Mental Disorders* (Third Edition)—known popularly as the "DSM III," published by the American Psychiatric Association, Washington, D.C., 1980. For a description of aggressive behavior, see especially Conduct Disorder, Aggressive, p. 47, Antisocial Personality Disorder (behavior prior to age 15), p. 320; for passive behavior, see Identity Disorder, pp. 65–67, Avoidant Disorder, pp. 53–55, Avoidant Personality Disorder, pp. 363–365, Overanxious Disorder, pp. 55–57, Major Depressive Episode, pp. 213–214, Dependent Personality Disorder, pp. 324–326, and Immature or Inadequate Personality Disorders, p. 330. We also use "passive" to represent non-assertive behavior, described in the works listed in the bibliography on assertiveness (at the end of Chapter V). For description of passive-aggressiveness, see Oppositional Disorder, pp. 63–65 and Passive-Aggressive Personality Disorder, pp. 328–329, of the DSM III.

To help a student, it is important first to individualize him, to see him as himself rather than as a faceless member of a crowd. When a teacher does not recognize the individual differences between students, he will see and respond to them as a vast undifferentiated ego mass, impossible to understand, control, or help. Conversely, when differences can be recognized, the problems in dealing with a class become manageable and solutions become evident. This is the first step in classic problem-solving:* to distinguish one problem from another. (My wife, who treats alcoholic veterans, tells me that World War II vets, who were assigned to "KP" in the days before the kitchen machines, report having felt overwhelmed when first confronted with mountains of potatoes—until they realized that they could only be held responsible for peeling one potato at a time. Then they were able to pick out a potato and start peeling—and no longer felt overwhelmed.)

Let us look more closely at the behavior choices that characterize these students.

The Aggressive Student

The aggressive student is the one who disrupts the teaching process by acting out in dramatic ways the painful feelings generated by his frustrations. He is

---

*See Chapter V in which Classic Problem-Solving is discussed as a teaching tool.

the one who is loudly and persistently challenging, who argues and disrespectfully "mouths off" and talks back. He bullies the teacher and his peers, is verbally and/or physically abusive and intimidating. He may be violent—a danger to himself or others. His fellow students and even his teacher may find him frightening. He may be a leader, because of his ability to frighten others into submission or because he has the temerity to act in ways that others would like to but don't dare. On the other hand, he may be a loner whom the others shun, viewing him as crazy or weird because of his extreme volatility and explosiveness.

The aggressive student has no appreciation for the rights of others. He has an impulse or need and immediately translates it into action, regardless of others and thoughtless of consequences; or he sees others as useful to him in getting his needs met, mere objects to be used in a primitive, direct, acting-out way. He usually knows only one way of coping with his impulses or needs: immediate aggression—attack. Waiting for gratification is something that doesn't occur to him and that he doesn't believe in—usually because it has seldom, if ever, worked for him. This is the student who fights, assaults, rapes, may even stab or shoot.

Case illustration: Students are coming to class. Some are kidding each other, there is some good-natured jostling, then they begin to take their seats and settle down. Suddenly Patrice bursts into the room. It is clear that he is upset, and he is making no attempt to hide that fact. His eyes flash and he glowers. He rummages noisily for the folder containing his work, finds it, and skins it at his desk. It hits the desk with a smack and the contents cascade over the desk and onto the floor. Rather than reach under the desk to pick them up, Patrice savagely kicks and shoves the desk which lurches into his neighbor who protests. Patrice grabs the other student by the shirt front and snarls at him through clenched teeth. They scuffle. The teacher moves in, sharply ordering Patrice to sit down. "Fuck you!" yells Patrice, and he runs out of the room.

The Passive Student

The passive student is the one who withdraws, who daydreams, sleeps, doesn't do his work, and is psychologically "not present." He may be a loner, or may be a follower. Usually he displays little energy, using it for his inner life. He may seem depressed and to have given up. He doesn't progress, but doesn't call attention to himself or require the teacher's time by disrupting the teaching process; so he may be overlooked or forgotten, lost in the shuffle. On the other hand, he may frustrate to distraction the conscientious or caring teacher who wants him to learn, or the controlling teacher who can't stand not to be obeyed.

The passive student has no concept of his own rights and has given up trying to get his needs met. He gives in to his peers and perhaps momentarily to his teachers, but hopes above all to be left alone. When their solitude is broken, some passive students may become frustrated to the point of erupting in a violent episode. However, the violence is isolated and not their characteristic mode of behavior.

Case illustration: Paul has no father: His mother was not married when Paul was born, and she has never talked about the man. As a matter of fact, she talks very little at all, being a withdrawn schizophrenic. Paul lived alone with his mother until his early school years, when he came to the attention of other adults who investigated the home situation and found that the little boy was caring for his nearly mute mother. For the next few years, Paul and his mother alternated between periods when she was in a psychiatric hospital and he was in a series of foster homes, and when both were home together. Foster homes didn't "take," partly because the placements were brief, and partly because Paul pined for his mother. With the substitute families he was tentative, always with his psychological bags packed and ready to leave, always longing for his mother. He made no friends, warmed to nobody, remained aloof—quiet, sad, polite, distant. Finally it was decided that the mother was too chronically ill and unreliable to be responsible for the boy, and Paul didn't go home again.

He is now in junior high, living like a temporary boarder in a foster home despite the fact that he has not lived at home with his mother for three years. He is an "underachiever" in school. He daydreams, doesn't concentrate on his work. His handsome face turns away, the dull eyes making no contact with others. He ignores his classmates, is formally courteous to adults. When not sitting quietly at his desk he can often be found standing in the supply closet, facing the wall while tears slide down his cheeks. If someone tries to comfort him, he stiffens and turns away. He is truly alone except for his thoughts of his mother, whom he asks about but about whom he

will not talk. One gets the impression he is drained of
energy. Perhaps it is all used up on his lonely inner life.
None is left over for the outside world.

The Passive-Aggressive Student

The passive-aggressive youngster is the manipulator. He gets his needs met, gets his kicks, by getting *others* to act out. He is the one who sets
emotional fires in the classroom, who instigates, up-
sets others, who plays "Let's you and him fight." He
is hard to identify because he may be a very slick
operator who silently pushes others' buttons to
watch them explode. He is an undercover
maneuverer. He may appear to be passive, but his
passivity is more a way of getting the teacher's goat
than of simply wanting to be left alone. It is usually
a "game."

The passive-aggressive student, like the aggressive student, has little or no respect for the rights of
others. Like the aggressive student, he uses others
to get his needs met, but in an indirect way. Peers
and teachers are treated as objects to be manipulated and outsmarted, rather than bullied outright or
directly overcome.

Case illustration: I watched a passive-aggressive eleven-
year-old operate one afternoon in a classroom of a small
private suburban elementary school. (I was observing
through a one-way window.) Some students in the class
were working at tables by themselves; others worked
quietly in irregular groups of two to four. There was gen-

eral movement as students got materials, sharpened pencils, checked each other's work, spoke with the teacher, shifted from one activity to another. The teacher walked around the classroom also. The atmosphere was one of quiet restlessness and absence of structure. Because of this, I did not at first notice Chuckie—he was sort of disguised by the movement, blending in with the underbrush, so to speak.

Chuckie prowled, quiet and graceful as a cat, from individual to group, peering over a shoulder here, making a remark or two there, barely alighting before twirling away to resume his ballet. As he would leave, however, he might pinch someone, dislodge some work, or somehow disrupt the concentration or comfort of the students. I watched for over an hour, and during that time Chuckie himself did no work at all.

For the most part, his peers ignored him, acting toward his little "hit-and-run" raids as if he were an annoying mosquito, a minor and momentary nuisance. Meanwhile, however, Chuckie was gradually increasing his momentum, feeding bit-by-bit on the gratification he was getting from this activity. His movements became quicker, more slapstick, but still he managed to avoid attracting the attention of the teacher. Although he had appeared at first to be innocently relaxed and oblivious of the teacher, actually he was sharply aware of where the teacher was and where his attention was directed at all times. He managed to stay on the "blind side" of the teacher most of the time—all of the time when he was making a "strike."

Finally he managed "accidently" to inflict a very painful blow on Eric, one of his peers. The hurt boy exploded with tears and righteous rage, and the teacher intervened. Chuckie, with an innocent smile, declared it was an accident. Eric knew better and furiously disputed it, lunging for Chuckie, who remained calm and just out of reach while the teacher protected him by restraining the "uncontrolled" Eric.

The teacher, unaware of Chuckie's role, talked earnestly to Eric, holding him by the shoulders. He was somewhat frustrated and annoyed, however, because Eric was not giving him complete attention: From behind the teacher's back, Chuckie was smirking at Eric, who helplessly glowered back. Eric knew that he was the victim of a deliberate and vicious attack, but he got nowhere with his efforts to obtain justice. The teacher told him "It's over. Settle down and shake hands." Chuckie, smiling held out his hand; Eric angrily rejected it, and refused to be placated. The teacher wandered off, but had to return shortly when Eric, being quietly goaded and taunted by Chuckie, tried to even the score.

The final outcome was that eight students, including Chuckie and Eric, were organized for a square dance rehearsal, but Eric was still so upset and angry from the unresolved episode that he was unable to participate. He ended up being isolated until he could get himself under control, whereas Chuckie enjoyed the square dance, occasionally shooting a sly smirk in Eric's direction.

Eric was never able to enlist the teacher's help in understanding what he was going through and finding a comfortable way to deal with it. Chuckie had had a "profitable" afternoon, having learned once again that he could get away with torturing someone, get some excitement and triumph, and avoid either academic work or learning how to deal better with his own angry feelings or with peer relationships. Although Chuckie got off scotfree that afternoon, one has a dismal feeling about the future. Eventually he will pay in ways that may be terribly sad and bewildering.

Meanwhile, the teacher, oblivious to it all, had tried to paper over the incident, thus missing a wonderful opportunity to help *both* boys. He had seen an outburst, interpreted it as a problem but not an opportunity, and tried to stop it. He had also seen Eric's behavior as the problem. Usually, when a passive-aggressive person is operating, the victim gets the blame.

The passive-aggressive student has greater capacity to wait for his payoff or gratification, so long as he is actively engaged in a plan or maneuver. If not allowed to maneuver, he may become explosive and aggressive, or (less often) depressed and withdrawn.

The "Normal" Student Who Acts Out or Becomes Withdrawn

Occasionally, a student who has a consistent history of normal adaptation to family, neighborhood, and school, who has developed well, related easily to others, progressed and achieved as expected, will unexpectedly go all to pieces, alternately withdrawing and acting-out, or flying into rages or simply becoming passive and defeated. This student is different from the others described above in that he has well-established and demonstrated strengths and an adequate variety of coping skills, but some overwhelming situational stress has overtaken him and short-circuited his ability to cope. This child is not unconcerned about self or others, may be sensitive and feel guilty, but not have the resources to deal with whatever is stressing him. His problem behavior is not a long-standing part of his character, but actually an anomaly, uncharacteristic of him.

See the case illustration in the next section (p. 32), describing the older of the two dyslexic boys. This boy was able to deal in a healthy manner with all aspects of his life except the circumscribed area dominated by his dyslexia. Only gradually did his

frustrated feelings begin to spread the problem behavior, until it contaminated other areas of his life.*
He acted out aggressively. In contrast, his sister responded to her stress by becoming withdrawn.

Such children respond positively to the approaches presented in this book because they still need special help in dealing with overwhelming stress—either arising from conditions within themselves (e.g., illness or disability), or from external sources (e.g., an episode of social or familial disruption). The difference is that they have a head start on the others because of their greater strength. They usually respond quickly, successfully overcome their difficulties, and maintain their success without relapse.

Since all these students behave differently, it follows that they need to be treated differently. They share general problems: (1) inaccessibility to the educational process (in their present state); (2) poverty of coping skills, and rigidity in clinging to one type of coping which is inadequate for their needs and for enabling them to grow; (3) collusion with each other in preserving their inadequate choices of coping; and (4) lack of (or inadequate) understanding and appreciation for self and others or of their own and others' rights.

To the extent that they are different, they require different approaches. To the extent that they are

---

*In this case, although the child had a normal personality, a disorder was present as a stressor: see Developmental Reading Disorder, p. 93–94 of DSM III.

alike, they can benefit from the same general approach, lending each other their strengths and sharing in the same healing process.

A Few Words About Causation

Sometimes too much is said about cause. It is not always possible to know the cause of behavior problems.* For example, much has been said over the years about the causal role of rigid or punitive toilet training, or the loss of a parent, or the dislocations of divorce. However, the role of "potty training" on later behavior is so speculative as to be generally useless, and many many children survive divorces and parental loss strongly intact.

Poor parenting used to be blamed as the "cause" of infantile autism, that most devastating and puzzling of childhood disabilities; now professionals aren't so sure. But many parents of autistic children suffered acutely—not only from the awfulness of their child's disorder, but also from the guilt they felt for having "caused" it. This is truly an example of "blaming the victim," and we would be wise not to go around placing blame when the "cause" is still wreathed in theory.

Sometimes the "cause" is too remote to do anything about anyway. ("So you were potty-trained

---

*The DSM III, for example, has generally avoided etiology, in favor of description of disorders, because of this problem of unknown causes and conflicting theories of causation.

wrong when you were three. What are you going to do about that now?") The problem is the present behavior, and it has to be dealt with here and now.

On the other hand, sometimes people make the mistake of treating the behavior and ignoring the underlying cause, when the cause is one that is discoverable, with the result that they are exhausting themselves in efforts to deal with symptoms which are being constantly stimulated by an active and powerful causative factor. They are like people frantically pulling drowning bodies out of a river, but who never think to send somebody upstream to see who is throwing them in!

There is much we don't know about the cause of behavior problems, but there are some notable causes that are known and can be diagnosed. Three obvious examples are (1) learning disabilities, (2) allergies, sugar, and food additives,* and (3) drug

---

*There is controversy about sugar and food additives, as well as allergies, as "causes" of behavior problems. However, because of widely-reported experience that children have been helped by diet change, we include them here despite the conflicting results of the research. The reader who wants to explore this further may want to refer to:

Jerome Vogel, M.D., *A Stress Test For Children—Is Your "Problem Child's" Problem Nutrition? Here's How to Find Out,* New Canaan, Conn.: Keats Publishing, 1983.
See the bibliography in this book by the Medical Director of the New York Institute for Child Development;
Lendon Smith, M.D., *Improving Your Child's Behavior Chemistry,* Englewood Cliffs, N.J.: Prentice-Hall, 1976.

Our own experience has been that diet and allergy treatment is helpful in some cases of behavior problems.

abuse. More will be said about drug abuse later in Chapter V ("Affective Education and Drug Abuse—A Special Issue"). Every child who comes to our attention because of behavior problems should be screened to rule out the possibility that any of these three factors may be causing or exacerbating the behavior.

Case illustration: I have friends, three of whose four children had dyslexia. After a normal, and socially outstanding older daughter, they had a girl who was bright and happy and sociable until she was in the third grade. Gradually, her behavior and personality changed until she became an anxious and depressed loner, a school failure. Nobody knew why, and speculated that the "cause" was the advent of a handsome baby brother, the "long-awaited boy," and that she was now a "middle" child, in limbo between a spectacular older sister and the new baby, with neither of whom she could successfully compete. Sensitive and caring, her parents gave her more attention, to the point of exhaustion, to prove to her that she was as valuable to them as the other children. Nothing worked, however, and the downward spiral continued. She spent a great deal of time in her room, depressed, staring at the ceiling. She was ridiculed by her peers, but couldn't seem to find the energy to deal with it.

Meanwhile another brother was born. The lives of the two boys began to take a turn similar to that of their sister: obviously bright, creative, sunny, well-adjusted children, they too began to change after a while in school. The older boy, previously outgoing, capable, and easily-managed, gradually began having episodes of rage and acute frustration, particularly related to math and his math teacher. A hard-working, conscientious boy, he spent hours on his math homework only to get it wrong, day after day. His teacher told him that the only reason he could be having such trouble, since he was so bright, was that he was *lazy*. Yet he knew he wasn't lazy. The incongruity of the explanation (viewed by him as an unfair accusation), coupled with the mysterious but stubborn failure, drove him wild. He began having explosive episodes in school and at home. One day he nearly destroyed his classroom.

By chance, the family moved during the time things were coming to a crisis, and a well-informed teacher at the new school suspected dyslexia. Tests confirmed the suspicion. The younger brother was tested and he had it too. (Dyslexia tends to "run in families.") The boys' problem was remediated, and the behavior problems abruptly stopped, never to reappear. But it was too late for the daughter, who was already through school, her misery long-standing and entrenched. It took years of courageous effort for her to achieve a measure of happiness.

It is folly to treat the behavior without giving whatever tests are known to be effective, to rule out an underlying treatable disorder. When the underlying disorder is remedied, often the child's own natural strength and good sense will take care of the rest. If the problem cannot be remedied, knowing of its impact will be helpful to the child and all concerned about him. They will not blame themselves and waste time and energy casting about for unworkable "remedies." The child will not think he is "crazy" or ruled by fearsome mysterious forces. If it takes significant time to effect a remedy, you will be able to use the knowledge presented here, but in the meantime you won't be working in a no-win situation.

How These Students Relate to Each Other: "Sliding Partners"

"Sliding Partner" is a term that has come to use from the indigenous culture of the jails, but it is not limited to the prison milieu. It describes a particular kind of relationship that exists not only in prisons but also on the streets, and is especially characteristic of youth with behavior disorders.

The "sliding partner" is a person who fleetingly shares an event for his own purposes. Seeing another behaving in an irresponsible or self-destructive manner, the sliding partner either moves in actively to encourage or support it, or stands by and allows it, passively supporting by not interfering with it. He does this because he gets something out of the other's behavior—perhaps vicarious "kicks," excitement, a "high," company in misery, or approval or "respect" from the other.

The sliding partner never "rats on" or confronts the person engaged in irresponsible or destructive behavior. Sliding partners help each other get away with something, then go their separate ways again. They are "passing acquaintances" of the most superficial sort, ensuring that they do not become entrapped into deeper relationships that might require sacrifice or loyalty or consistency, or "facing the music." Often the participants will glamorize the sliding partner relationship, trying to endow it with a depth it doesn't have, calling each other, "My Main Man," or "brother," or "buddy." Do not be deceived!

Sometime ago I worked with fighting street gangs in San Francisco. What I was reading at that time by the sociologists and social workers indicated that gang members were bound together by deep loyalties and trust, formalized by a gang code. What I found in actuality was a gang code, all right; but rather than depth of concern and trust I found a shifting kaleidoscope of loosely structured relationships bound together by a common turf, a name, danger, and a false "honor," that encouraged illegal behavior by mutually protecting each other and egging each other on. A gang is simply a discrete collection of sliding partners. Surprisingly, so is a classroom or a school playground—often!

Case illustration: Children are running, playing, shouting on the school playground at recess. Suddenly a knot forms that has a different quality to it, a different sound, a different rhythm of motion. Others are attracted to the spot. A fight has broken out between two students. The others watch, shouting encouragement; a few ignore it, going about their own business. Soon a faculty member comes on the scene, shouting sternly above the din, shouldering students aside. He stops the fight. A few students take sides with the antagonists, proclaiming their innocence. The teacher says he will take care of the problem. He disperses the crowd and marches the battlers into the building.

The students who stood by and watched without trying to get the fight stopped, the students who egged the fighters on, and those who tried to take sides to protect the fighters, were all sliding partners. The adult, by taking the responsibility on his own shoulders without involving the others in problem-solving toward a solution to fighting, effectively protected and maintained the conditions in which sliding partnerships can flourish, and thus ensured that this way of relating would continue.

Case illustration: Sliding Partners who actively encourage irresponsible behavior: The physical education teacher had a pair of gym shorts lying on his desk. They were unlike the regulation shorts, which were quite plain. This particular pair of shorts had been donated to the gym teacher by somebody, and they were handsome—satin with contrasting satin trim.

A few days later, the shorts were missing from the teacher's desk, but showed up on Jared in gym class. The teacher accosted the resplendent Jared, telling him to go to the locker room, take off the shorts, and put on the regulation uniform.

"What for?" snapped Jared, elaborately astounded.

"Because those are mine, the ones that were on my desk."

"No they aren't! I brought these from home!" protested Jared, affronted.

"Yeah! That's right Coach! He brought 'em from home. I seen him," piped up a sliding partner, moving in swiftly.

"Yeah. He brought 'em from home!" stated several others, menacingly, gathering around. They are sliding partners. Ordinarily they are not known for being friends. They are taking this opportunity actively to encourage and support Jared for reasons of their own.

Case illustration: Sliding Partners who passively allow or passive-aggressively encourage irresponsible behavior: Sal has a history of assaulting teachers. Until this year, he managed to walk a thin line just this side of being suspended from school. For example, he would hang around the hall, chronically late for class, and if a teacher touched his arm, saying, "Come on, Sal, let's get to class," Sal would respond in a surly but soft voice (while moving obediently toward the classroom) "Get your hands off me, man, I can get myself to class."

In recent months, however, his behavior is changing; now he overtly rebels. His folder is full of reports of assaults and obscene language directed at faculty. Faculty are afraid of him, and avoid him. Sal roams the halls by himself, glaring, banging lockers with a wrench picked up from shop class, generally intimidating anyone who is in the vicinity. His peers either watch silently as he holds sway, or they give him a signal with body-language such as a "power sign" or a pat on the back. They are passive sliding partners.

So long as the student can continue successfully to have sliding partners, or be a sliding partner, it is almost impossible to reach him, to get him to take responsibility for his behavior and to change it. The task of the teacher who hopes to get his students to relate to each other in a responsible, meaningful, healthy way, is to change the setting in such a way as to inhibit or interfere with or prevent the development of sliding partnerships, and simultaneously to provide opportunities that demand the development of deep, caring, unsuperficial relationships. To do this requires creating an altogether different milieu—a caring milieu.

By far the most effective way I have found to do this involves the creation of peer triads, which are described in detail beginning with Chapter IV. In the triads, each student must relate consistently and intensely with two other students. Intrusion into the triad is limited by the structure. Authority problems and rebelliousness are obviated, by the encouragement of the opportunity to impress his peers (by positive rather than negative behavior, for a change).

Until the triads can be set up and begin to function, however, the teacher will need to interfere actively with the acting-out student who stimulates sliding partnerships. This problem is dealt with in the next chapter.

Suggested Readings

Erikson, Erik. *Childhood and Society*. New York: W. W. Norton, 1950.

Harshman, Hardwick W. (ed.). *Educating the Emotionally Disturbed, A Book of Readings*. New York: Thomas Y. Crowell, 1969.

Redl, Fritz, and Wineman, David. *Children Who Hate, The Disorganization and Breakdown of Behavior Controls*. New York: The Free Press, 1951.

2. First Things First: Curing Chaos—Control of the Aggressive Student

Disturbing the peace is as serious a matter in school as it is on the street—perhaps even more serious. No effective learning and teaching can take place where discipline breaks down.

Mortimer Adler
The Paideia Proposal

Why the Aggressive Student?

No teaching can take place in chaos. Of the three types of student described in the last chapter, the aggressive student is the one who presents the immediate problem. It is *he* who completely disrupts the education process and prevents you from teaching. The passive student may frustrate your need for accomplishment, your need to see results from your efforts to help him. And the passive-aggressive student may annoy you and others with his stubborn resistance—but if nobody reacts to him, he can't get his game going effectively because he generally needs somebody to play his game with him.

But the aggressive student, all by himself, can make a shambles of a classroom in a moment. So, unlike the WW II soldier doing K.P., all of whose potatoes were essentially the same, it is important for a teacher to pick the right "potato" to deal with first: the explosive, aggressive, disruptive, acting-out student.

The Purpose of Control

The first thing that must be understood in establishing a caring classroom is that no learning, growing, and caring can take place without control. The absence of control is chaos.

The immediate goal of control is to enable you to teach. The ultimate goal is to create an atmosphere in which each student can eventually gain inner control, so that he can take responsibility for his own learning and his own life. Control is not an end in itself; we teachers are not in the business of controlling but of educating. Control of one person by another is only a good thing as a beginning. An example would be a parent who controls the dangerous impulses of a two-year-old to run across the street, but who eventually transfers that control to the now older child who can cross the street responsibly by himself. The contrast would be the case of the unrehabilitatable psychopath who must be controlled by bars and armed guards all his life because he is a threat to others; that is not the business of the teacher.

It is imperative that the teacher have control over himself, over the classroom (that is, the teaching process and how it takes place), and over the students until such time as the students have gained control over themselves and can behave responsibly. Then, control can be shared.

Unless the teacher clearly understands the process by which people change, he will be tempted to misuse control. There are basically two ways that people change: (a) they change themselves, or (b) they are changed by others. The first way is the way of freedom and responsibility; the second is not free, and the person being changed becomes an object upon which various acts are performed. Examples of methods by which people are changed by others are: coercive force, manipulating, and behavior modification.

In a caring classroom, students are taught to treat each other with respect. One cannot respect someone and treat him as an object simultaneously. Thus, the purpose of this program is to create a situation within which the student is able to change himself. If the teacher doesn't believe in self-change, and really prefers to exert force on others to change them, he will have a difficult time with the method described in this book, and will lapse into coercion and manipulation, and "Rescuing" (about which more will be said in a later section).

In addition to the ethical issues involved in changing other people, there are the practical issues of energy expenditure and overwhelming responsibility. If the teacher proposes to change others, he must create a system of continual force, in which everybody, from the teacher down through every member of the class, acts upon those weaker than he—weaker either in will-power, or in motivation to exert one's will on another, or in energy for this particular goal. The gentler members of the class will not make themselves felt. Further, the *teacher* will be responsible for all the changing (a heavy weight to carry), rather than for creating, with helpers, an atmosphere within which growth can take place.

When students change themselves, the teacher neither takes the blame nor the credit. If he has done his job, the student is free to change. If the student chooses not to change, that is *his* choice and *his* responsibility. If he does change, *he* can take the credit and the teacher can applaud and respect him (and the teacher can respect himself for having provided the opportunity). For those familiar with Transactional Analysis terminology, the process in which one person changes another is characterized by "I'm OK, you're not OK," and the process by which a person is enabled to change himself is represented as "I'm OK—You're OK." The latter is by far the more comfortable for all concerned.

The teacher who controls a student is telling him: "Your *behavior* is not OK and I cannot allow you to continue hurting yourself and others this way; but since *you* are OK, I will control you only until you can control yourself, and I am confident that you will soon be able to." This is a very different message from "I'm OK, and stronger and better than you; you are not OK and never will be, on your own. Therefore I will control you now, and then I will change you until I have made you into what I want you to be."

A "Contract" with the Administrator

Purpose of the Contract. Teachers do not work in a vacuum and classrooms do not exist in a vacuum. During the initial period of establishing control over the disruptive student (the beginning stage of establishing a caring classroom), the teacher's job is made either immensely easier or immensely harder by support or lack of support from the administrator. Acquainting the administrator with your goals and techniques and getting his support will be well worth the expense of time and effort. If you will be using the model presented in this book, it will be to your advantage if your administrator has read it, and/or you have discussed together the concepts and tools of the model; the hope is to share a common understanding of your goals and methods.

The teacher in the throes of struggling with one or more students for control needs all his energy, at that time, for that process. Any energy drained off in impromptu explanations to the administrator, or in fending off challenges by the administrator to the teacher's autonomy, or in undoing the damage caused by well-meaning administrators who are operating from an entirely different philosophy, weakens the teacher's effectiveness and may seriously damage or at least postpone the possibility of success.

I am not saying that you cannot be successful without the understanding, cooperation, and support of your administrator; I am saying only that your job will be much harder and the process much slower. If you and your administrator act as a team, each complementing the other, you will both be stronger. Therefore, take the time *first,* before getting into the thick of it with the students, to get to know each other professionally, and explore how you can help each other to meet each other's goals.

What You Want From Your Administrator. It is imperative that the students see, demonstrated, the potency of the teacher. If the teacher does not have control over his own domain, decision, and actions, the students will soon see this and discount him. Therefore, the teacher should not be publicly countermanded by the administrator. In other words, you must be able to convince the student that *you* will and can control him, for him, until he is able to control himself.

If he observes the teacher's control being challenged successfully by the administrator, that the teacher cannot follow through on what he says, or has to spend his time convincing the administrator, the student will not believe or trust in the teacher's ability to control him, and he will have to keep testing to see whether or not he can rely on the teacher. If he finds he cannot rely on the teacher (the teacher cannot control him), there is no hope left; and the teacher has been rendered impotent.

Noninterference. Tell your administrator that you are seeking an agreement that he will generally trust in your knowing what you are doing, even if he doesn't understand what he observes at a given moment. Remember, however, that trust is earned. You will be trusted only if you have built up a reputation for competence, or if you have taken the time to develop a mutual respect for and agreement with each other's goals. Nobody should demand a carte blanche for trust without establishing a basis for it, and no administrator worth his salt would give such trust.

Ask your administrator, if he strongly disagrees with or doesn't understand an action you have taken, to discuss it with you in private, and to give you the opportunity to explain and if appropriate to effect any changes that may be called for by the discussion. In other words, if you are overruled, you make the correction—not the administrator. Make sure he understands how important it is that he never overrule you in front of the students.

You also have *your* obligations under this clause in the contract: Such noninterference presupposes that you will always be in control of yourself and will never do anything harmful to the students. Hitting, bullying, and ridiculing of students is never acceptable behavior for a teacher. ("Never" is an absolute term, and the use of absolutes generally is dangerous, but I believe it is warranted here.) Hitting, bullying, and ridiculing of students by a teacher should not be tolerated by an administrator.*

Physical *punishment* of a student by a teacher should be interfered with immediately by the administrator. Just as the student who aggresses against another person is out-of-control and needs to be controlled, the teacher who aggresses against another person is out-of-control and needs to be controlled. The administrator has a responsibility to do that.

However, it is important for both the teacher and the administrator to understand the difference between physical *punishment* or *aggression* by a teacher—which are not to be condoned—and physical *restraint* of a student by a teacher—which may be necessary to keep the student from harming himself or others, and thus may be a therapeutically necessary intervention at the moment. One of the most therapeutic experiences an out-of-control child can have is to learn that there is an adult who can control him in a caring way.

There is one more form of non-interference you will want to ask for: an agreement that the administrator and others not "visit" or "observe" your classroom during this beginning stage of gaining control. The less outside stimulation there is, the easier it

---

*For more on this, see "They're Asking for It," by D. J. Carducci, in *The American Teacher*, Feb., 1972.

will be for you and the students during this high-energy, stressful time.

Sometimes students play to the gallery, and sometimes teachers are especially uncomfortable, when they are being observed. Teachers may think they are being "judged" when the class is not at its best. During this stage the classroom may be noisy or there may be outbursts. This is not the time to contend with feelings of being on display, or self-consciousness, or need to be hospitable. These same noisy outbursts may also bring "rescuing"* colleagues or administrators to your door to "help." Explain ahead of time that if you need help you will ask for it.

You have responsibilities under this clause in the contract as well: You will give the administrator as much time, explanation, discussion, information, and problem-solving effort as he wants, in private at a convenient time, so that he can do *his* job and discharge *his* responsibility. After initial control has been established, anyone may visit your classroom at any time. (I have a table in my classroom for observers.)

A "Holding" or "Time-Out" Area Away From the Classroom. Explain to the administrator that your goal is to deal with the problems within the classroom, in contrast to the popular practice of expelling problem students or "dumping" them on somebody

---

*See Chapter V, p. 148 below, on "rescuing."

else (usually the administrator or an "expert"). You will not be "sending students to the office" to be disciplined or otherwise "dealt with" by the administrator.

However, in the early stages of gaining control, occasionally (sometimes often) one or more students may need to be removed from the classroom for a period of time.* Ask for an area (a separate room if possible, a place to sit down in the administrative offices if there is no other place available), to be designated as your "holding" room or area.

If you have a "holding room," you will need an aide who is under your supervision to supervise the students who are sent there. If you have only an area of the administrative offices, such as the waiting area, and the administrator is therefore overseeing the student you have sent there, be sure the administrator understands and accepts your philosophy and goals for your use of this area.**

---

*For an explanation of how to use this technique, see Chapter III, D, below.

**If you do not have a holding room, or an aide, or a supportive administrator, I have found it useful to have an agreement with a fellow teacher that we can send students to each other's time-out areas within our classrooms. (See Chapter III, p. 64 below, for details of the "time-out" area.) Usually a student is much more subdued and less apt to act-out with an unfamiliar teacher in an unfamiliar room. It is useful in such instances to tell your students that you have this arrangement, and tell them where the time-out area is in the other teacher's room; then, if you have to use it, you save the student some embarrassment: you can take him to the door, but he walks in unaccompanied and goes to the time-out area without escort.

No teacher or administrator, or any other support or ancillary adult is to get involved in any discussion with a student in a holding room or area. They are to listen to no excuses or explanations, nor are they to do any "problem-solving" with the student. Those activities are reserved for you, and the student is to be told that he must deal with you. If necessary, the adults are to "broken-record" this response to attempts by the student to involve them in the problem. ("You need to discuss that with your teacher." "Look, you're going to have to deal with your teacher about that.")

There is a very good reason for stressing the importance of the other adults not getting involved. It will be described in more detail later, but briefly it is this: Most acting-out youngsters are masters at excusing their own behavior and projecting blame for it onto others. Their problem was with you, and only you know the particulars. You are responsible for resolving the problem with the student. If the student gets an opening, he will seduce the unsuspecting "helping" adult into an endless stream of excuses, red herrings, rationalizations, accusations that you have been unfair, and pleas of innocence—until the whole process is so diluted, muddied, and convoluted that your hope of getting him to face up to responsibility for his own behavior will be all but lost.

Keep it simple: The problem is between him and you; all others stay out! They are there only to keep order, not to get involved.

Your Part of the Contract. In return for these agreements on the part of the administrator, you will deliver in due time a genuinely caring classroom, in which students who have been disrupting the school will instead be learning, and in which problems are resolved without the need to encroach on the administrator's time and energy. You will also, during this process, work as closely with the administrator as he wishes, to keep him informed of what you are doing and why. You will be open, direct, and assertive in discussing the administrator's concerns about what you are doing, and in problem-solving with him, and will be cooperative in arriving at necessary solutions.

If you are an inexperienced teacher in the process of earning the administrator's confidence, you will probably be working in a closer, more supervisee-supervisor relationship. This need not stop you from asking for the opportunity to correct your own mistakes rather than have them corrected for you. If you and the administrator share the same goals of concern for the students' behavior and for effective education, the chances are good that you can work out a satisfactory contract with each other.

Case illustration: Mike, a young rather inexperienced teacher, was asked to serve as a substitute teacher of a class of disturbed institutionalized teenaged girls. On entering the room he discovered that there was no lesson plan. The girls seemed to be calm, talking quietly among themselves. However, when he gave them three choices of things they could do during the period, they objected, saying they were going to spend the class time talking

with each other, and that he should "buzz off." He
pressed the issue, and they began to yell insults at him.
One very volatile girl began screaming, grabbed a chair
and heaved it in his direction. It struck the wall and
broke. Mike grabbed the girl and pinned her arms.
Another teacher, hearing the noise, came into the room.

Mike asked the teacher to stay with the class while he
took the chair-heaver to the "holding room." After leaving her in the "holding room," he returned to the class.
However, the girls continued to riot, yelling, surrounding
him, and grabbing at his pants. He became anxious. He
left the class and told the principal that the entire group
was out of control and should be removed from the building until conferences could be held.

Instead the principal dismissed him and took the class
himself, spending the time in discussion with the girls
about "why" they had behaved the way they had. The
girls immediately became deeply involved in a discussion
about Mike. By the end of the period the girls were calm,
they and the principal "understood each other," and Mike
had been rendered impotent. Mike asked for a conference
with the principal to discuss the incident and was told
that one would be arranged, but it never was. Mike felt
angry, frustrated, discounted, and at a great disadvantage
in any future conflict with the students. (Word gets
around quickly.)

Furthermore, an important opportunity was missed:
Because administrators have powers that teachers do not
have, they can step into problem situations like this and
"take care" of them. The students are often sufficiently in
awe of the administrator's power, also, to defer to him
where they would not defer to a teacher—as happened in
this case.

Here, the administrator used the power inherent in his
position to discredit the teacher, who lacked power for
several reasons: (1) young and inexperienced, he probably appeared to the students to be somewhat less than

totally confident; (2) he was a substitute, with no experience or relationship or prior "position" with the group; and (3) he had no agreement with the administrator that he would be supported by the administrator's power (a lending of power).

By using his power instead of lending it, the administrator missed a very important opportunity to mold a young teacher—to help him acquire legitimate power of his own. If the administrator had restrained himself in his temptation to get a "quick settlement," he could have assisted the young teacher in solving his own problem, and thereby increased his confidence, his fund of useful experience, and his potency with the students.

Suggested Readings

Bettelheim, Bruno. *Surviving, and Other Essays.* New York: Alfred A. Knopf, 1979. See especially the chapter entitled "Education and the Reality Principle," pp. 127–141.

Carducci, Dewey J. "They're Asking For It," *The American Teacher,* American Federation of Teachers, Feb., 1972.

Long, Nicholas, Morse, William C., and Newman, Ruth G. (eds.). *Conflict in the Classroom: The Education of Emotionally Disturbed Children.* Belmont, Calif.: Wadsworth, 1965.

Redl, Fritz, and Wineman, David. *Controls From Within, Techniques for the Treatment of the Aggressive Child.* New York: The Free Press, 1952.

3. Tools for Gaining Control, and How to Use Them

*A*s described above, you cannot begin to do anything constructive with your class so long as one or more aggressive students are out of control and making your class into a disaster area. Therefore you must bring disruptive students under your control. There are tools that have been proven useful in this process. They are:

a. obtaining a commitment by the student to change his behavior,
b. a "time-out" area within the classroom,
c. positive peer pressure,
d. removal from the classroom to a "holding" room or area, and
e. the last-resort conference.

The Commitment to Change *

Aggressive students know that what they are doing is unacceptable, but they seldom if ever have really thought about it, because of the way adults usually respond to their behavior. Adults tend to have several stock responses, none of which is helpful to the student in bringing about acceptable behavior. Adults have either:

- *punished* him (become counter-aggressive)—which only proves that aggressive behavior is OK so long as you are the stronger antagonist ("might makes right"); or
- asked him for an *explanation*—which has enabled him to excuse his behavior on the basis of his having been a victim (adults are often pushovers for a sad story about family deprivation, or will allow themselves to be led down the garden path by involved stories of how the teacher mistreated him—"so what else could you expect?"—or of how other students set him up—"so I had to act the way I did."); or
- teachers have been *intimidated* by him—which has proved to him that he can get what he wants (power, or money, or to be left alone . . .) by being aggressive.

Such responses only serve to reinforce or justify the student's bad choice of behavior. And especially

---

*For background on the concept of commitments, see William Glasser, *Reality Therapy, op. cit.*

they do not present the student with an acceptable alternative coping behavior. What is particularly striking about children with behavior disorders is not so much the presence of unacceptable behavior as the absence of acceptable behavior. They don't know what to do instead!

The commitment to change is the first step in beginning to correct this problem: For the first time the student is expected to (1) face the fact that *his* behavior is unacceptable, (2) discuss acceptable alternatives, and (3) make a commitment to choose an alternative and act in an acceptable manner. (This is the beginning of his developing inner controls.)

Why "Commitment"? There is an old saying: "Promises are for kids—easily made and easily broken." Most people, even disturbed students, appreciate that a "commitment" is different from a promise. They will take it more seriously. It hooks into whatever code of honor they have, no matter how rudimentary. They will make a more serious effort to live up to a "commitment." It smacks of maturity.

How Do You Get the Commitment?

First: Make a quick decision—is the student so out of control that you can't talk with him? Your first step may need to be stopping the aggressive behavior. (This will depend on whether he is "building up" to aggressive behavior, such as verbal challenging— in which case you may be able to talk with him; or whether he is already in the midst of uncontrolled behavior such as throwing objects—in which case talking is, for the moment, pointless.)

If you must stop the behavior, do it firmly with only as much force as is necessary. Do not punish or hurt, physically or verbally. If you have the student in a grip, *his* thrashing around may result in his hurting himself, but you must be careful that *you* don't hurt him. If you are not big and strong enough to subdue him yourself, ask for help. Some of his peers may be trusted to help you. (Later on, as will be discussed in another section, the peers will be *expected* to exert this kind of control, but, in the initial stages, that may be too much to expect or you may not know them well enough to ask for their help.) You may ask other teachers in the vicinity, or the administrator or school guards (euphemistically, the "security personnel") to assist you.

Second: Once the student is under control (either in the classroom or outside of it), or before he has gotten completely out of control, tell him that what he is doing is unacceptable, and ask him what he plans on doing differently.* Usually the student will do everything he can to avoid the idea that *his* behavior is unacceptable. He will argue, project blame, in a frantic attempt to excuse his behavior and get you thinking and talking about something else. Your task

---

*This approach is described at length in William Glasser's book, *Reality Therapy.*

is not to accept any excuses or follow any red herrings. Tell him that your job is to teach, and you are not going to allow him to interfere with that. Do not get into an argument or discussion. Use as few words as possible. Repeat your question about what he is going to do differently.

Third: He probably won't have any idea of what he could do differently. He has only one way of coping, and the idea of changing will be a brand new concept to him. He will be confused, puzzled, and "stuck," and resentful. You will need to offer some alternatives. Example: "The next time you begin to get angry or upset, tell me before you lose your cool so I can help you with it. Do you understand that? Will you do it?" Wait for some acknowledgment. If there is some, accept it and leave it at that. Let him cool off. Get back to your classroom activities.

Sometimes you may opt to see if you can delay this entire discussion. You may say to the student, "I can see you are angry and I'm not sure what about. Will you cool it until after class when I can talk with you individually?" This is asking for a commitment (to "cool it") for a limited time, until you can help him deal with the problem more fully and give him your undivided attention. If he agrees, continue teaching.

(Note: He may have to use all his energy to "cool it" until you have time to talk with him. You do not need to feel guilty or uncomfortable if he does nothing else until you can get to him. He may read a magazine, put his head down on the table, sleep, or stare out the window; anything so long as he is not disruptive. The immediate goal (his control) has been reached and this is a victory for both of you. That is good enough for now.)

Do Not Use, or Allow the Students to Use, the Words *Why, Should,* **or** *Try. Why, should* and *try* are invitations to endless excuses and failure. Whenever you ask a student, "Why did you do that?" you are inviting him to regale you with all his rationalizations. Prepare to spend the next few months listening to them and getting nowhere.

If you say he "should" or "should not" do something, he may agree with you. So what? He is not making a *commitment* to do it or not do it. It is the same as saying to a heavy smoker, "You should stop smoking," and he replies (while lighting up another cigarette), "You're right, I really should." The smoker will not stop smoking because you and he have agreed that he *"should"*. He will stop only when he has made a firm decision, a "commitment" to himself, that he *will*. It is the same with the student. You and he can talk endlessly and amicably about what he "should" do, and he will never get around to changing.

"Try" is similar. Do an experiment and you will see that to "try" is to fail: Tell a friend or colleague to take a book that you hand him. Then ask him to "try" to toss it back to you. He will look a little puzzled, but will toss it to you. Tell him, "No, you didn't do what I told you. You tossed it to me. I told you to '*try*' to toss it to me." He will look even more puzzled and will make some motions as if to toss it to you but will actually be stopping himself from being successful in tossing it.

To "try" is to stop short of actually making a commitment. It is to "hedge," to hold back, to hold onto the idea in the back of one's mind that, "I probably will not be successful, but that's OK because I knew all along I wouldn't be able to do it." If your student says he will "try" to do the alternative, ask him what he means by try. Say, "Will you do it or won't you?" Put him on the spot. It may be that he doesn't want to do it, or that he doesn't think he can. If the latter, you may need to find a simpler alternative, or ask him to do the acceptable behavior for a short time-span so he can experience success and demonstrate that he can do it.

Positive Peer Pressure

This is a tool which works best *after* you have established a caring classroom, when new aggressive students come into it. As suggested above, if you don't know any of the class, or you know that none of them can be expected to use this tool appropriately, or you know that none of them understands yet how to give positive peer pressure, you cannot use this tool.

If you do have some reliable students, however, you could use it this way: First, stop the class. Address the whole group: "I wonder if others are bothered by John's behavior. It seems to me he is making it rough for the whole class." If there is no acknowledgment, discontinue and deal with the student without the peers. If there is agreement with your statement, ask for suggestions from the peers as to alternatives. One acceptable suggestion might be that a couple of his classmates take John to the "time-out" area (see below) and talk with him. Another (if your school is in an institution) might be that the group hold a meeting back at the cottage after school and that John "cool it" until then. (Again, as in the case where you delay talking with the student until after class, do not feel uncomfortable if the student does nothing other than control himself until the meeting with the peers takes place.)

Accept anything the peers suggest that is at all reasonable and that results in the aggressive student's coming under control. Your goals are simple: Get him under control and get back to teaching.

The "Time-Out" Area in the Classroom

Whenever possible, when the timing is appropriate, you want to deal with problems within the classroom, without removing the students, and involving as few other people as possible.* There are good reasons for this: (a) it establishes your potency with the students, demonstrating to them that you (and eventually they) can solve your own problems; (b) it

---

*For comments on timing, see p. 67.

keeps things simple;* too many extraneous elements (people or locations) begin not only to dilute the impact of what you are doing with the student, but also begin to sap your energy, because you have to deal with all the elements in order to keep things under control and moving toward your goal.

To facilitate dealing with problems within the classroom, establish a "time-out" area in the room, usually in a back corner. Cordon it off or separate it somehow by furniture arrangement so it can be recognized as a discrete area. This area is to be used whenever possible, as a preferable alternative to removing a disruptive student from the room.

Any student who is beginning to show signs of losing control is asked to go to the time-out area. Soon, students will recognize the usefulness of this area and will go there without your suggestion, to get themselves under control. I have had situations in which students have come to class already upset by some prior event and have gone directly to the time-out area for awhile of their own volition. (Note: You may find a student overusing the area. That is another problem to be dealt with separately. See Chapter V.)

In gaining initial control, after you have sent a misbehaving student to the time-out area, tell him to remain there until he is ready to make a commitment to change his behavior. When he decides that he is

---

*A good motto to have is to Keep It Simple, for yourself and for the students. When matters get too complicated or too hard to understand, they are usually beginning to fall apart.

ready to do that, he can quietly return to his seat, and you will talk with him at your convenience, either later in the class period or after class—but as soon as possible, because he will be under some stress to control himself, is making an effort, and deserves your earliest support.

A note about equipment in the "time-out" area: This is not a place for rest and relaxation, nor for entertainment, nor for academic work. Do not suggest that a student take his classwork back there. (The reason for this will be seen in the next chapter.) There should be no books or games, magazines, or other distractions. It is an area that you and the students respect as a place for thinking and considering better alternatives, for putting all available energy into gaining self-control.* (I have sometimes called this area the "Get-Yourself-Together Corner.")

The Holding Area

Occasionally, particularly early in the development of the caring milieu, it will be necessary and important to remove a student altogether from your classroom. In preparation for this, you have already

---

*This is not a contradiction to the Note to Reader on p. 61. In that case, the student has already made a commitment to the teacher to control himself and is not in the time-out area. He may read a magazine if that is helping him to control himself (by distracting him from the problem he can't yet deal with).

discussed a contract with the administrator (p. 45). The Holding Room or Area is only to be used when extreme measures are needed (as when a student is breaking up your room and refuses to be controlled in the classroom) or when none of the alternatives suggested above proves workable.

Use of the Holding Area is especially appropriate and important when you are just beginning with a new class and have not yet been able to establish an effective caring milieu. The students are not yet able to exert enough pressure on a disruptive student to contain him, and all the force of his violence is thus your unshared responsibility. At such a time you are truly still working alone. Yet your job is to teach, not to spend all your energy wrestling over an extended period with a student bent on disruption, chaos, or overpowering you. If you attempt to handle this alone, within the classroom, you are setting yourself up for some very bad results.

Case illustration: Arthur is a rather tense teacher whose esteem of order borders on rigidity; so he is perhaps more vulnerable to aggression than others (although we all have a breaking point). He is also very sensitive to how he is viewed by authority; being approved of and thought adequate by the principal is of major importance to him. He found himself contending with a foul-mouthed, taunting, aggressive girl who was successfully making a shambles of his class. He felt an obligation to deal with her himself, within the classroom, and did not make use of the available Holding Area. The other students sat back to watch the developments, curious about what the outcome would be. It was a duel between him and the girl.

The outcome was that he completely lost his composure one day. He first shouted to her to "SIT DOWN!" This was met by a challenge from her, and in trying to sit her down he went out of control, blackening her eye and clawing her around the neck.

Arthur's reluctance to use the Holding Area is shared by many teachers. They view it as a violation of "the code." Many teachers feel that they are (and they may actually be) evaluated on how well they control their class, handling everything themselves, never letting a problem trouble anyone else. They therefore resist letting a problem get out of their class, into the outer environment which is not so predictable and may involve them in criticism or interference, and where the situation may slip out of their hands. Such teachers feel very uncomfortable and guilty using the holding room, seeing its use as a sign of weakness and failure on their part. (This is why it is so important to have a contract with the administrator—so you both understand and support the need and rationale for the Holding Area).

If you find yourself troubled by such thoughts, dismiss them as irrational. Put them aside as fantasies of grandiosity, or needs to compensate for doubts about your adequacy. Realistically consider the resources you have to meet the challenge, and consider your priorities for your time and energy— and your responsibility to protect the educational process and attend to the other students.

If your resources include an established classroom, in which the other students are allies in containing the out-of-control student, then the chances are you will not need to use the Holding Area. But when you have not yet developed these resources, it may still be necessary to use it, and it is intelligent and appropriate to do so. If you are going to reassure a student that you are going to control him until he can control himself, you'd better be sure you can do it. If you can't, your attempt at reassurance will have deteriorated into an embarrassing loss of credibility, reinforcing the student's delusion that nobody can control him and he is all-powerful.

When you do decide to use the Holding Area, use it firmly. Say, "Look, I can't let you disrupt this class and steal your peers' education. If you can't control yourself, I'm going to have to control you, *for* you until you can! Nothing else seems to be working, so you make a decision: Either get hold of yourself or I'm going to take you to the Holding Area."

If you have already taken him there, kicking and screaming all the way, wait until he has calmed down enough to listen, and then tell him that he is to stay in the Holding Area (under supervision by an administrator or your aide or colleague), until he is ready to make a commitment to control himself enough to return to the classroom and not disrupt it. At the earliest possible time he is to be allowed back into his room. He may need some more time after that in your Time-Out area. That is OK. Use your judgment.

Remember that the Holding Area is *only* for the purpose of dramatizing the need for making a commitment to stop aggressive behavior, and only when the student is not able to make such a commitment without its use. You use it *only* when, in your judgment, none of the tools for use inside the classroom will work, and *only* to impress on the student the need for him to make a commitment to change his behavior in order to return to the class. It is *not* used as a means of getting rid of an annoyance, *not* to "dump" a problem on somebody else, *not* to "show him who's boss," and *not* for convenience. You are to remain involved with the student, and all your effort is directed at control and getting him back to class.

The "Last Resort Conference"

What if the student stays in the Holding Area without making a commitment, thinking that he can use this as a means of avoiding you and an education? Or what if he leaves the area and even the school building altogether? That is time to call a conference of the responsible adults (parents, or surrogate parents, or—if he is in an institution—cottage staff, social worker or other members of the treatment team).

The teacher maintains control of the conference by keeping the focus on the unacceptable behavior, acceptable alternatives, and how to get the student back into class. Occasionally a parent or other participant may begin to criticize the teacher. In such instances, the teacher refocusses by declining to be defensive and by commenting on the irresponsible manner in which the student is dealing with whatever the other adult thinks is wrong with the teacher.

In other words, nothing that the teacher has done or not done justifies the student's disrupting the educational environment. The focus is never to be allowed to be on the teacher or the teacher's behavior. This conference is about the *student's* irresponsible behavior and how the student can be helped to change it.

The change expected is very limited, namely that he agree to stop his uncontrolled behavior and return to the classroom. Your position is that he cannot return to the classroom until he is ready to make a commitment not to disrupt it. The student may be sent home (or, if in an institution, back to the cottage) for counseling by parents, caseworker, or cottage staff, whichever is revelant. He returns to class as soon as he is ready to talk with you about what he is ready to do differently. However, you may consult with him before that time, to offer suggestions as to what you will accept as alternative behavior.

Case illustration: Alonzo was a rough, tough, swaggering, handsome, streetwise, 15-year-old who was used to dealing with new situations by immediately trying to exert his dominance over others—usually with success in the school environment. He had left a bleak trail of wreckage throughout his school history, before he wound up in my special classroom in an institution for court-committed delinquents. His school records indicated that although he had normal intelligence, he read at a second grade level, so his use of energy in school had not served him well (although Alonzo thought that what he'd been doing was working for him).

His first few minutes in my class went very quickly. He came into the room already in the midst of a conflict with a classmate. I could see them glowering at each other. Within moments, Alonzo loudly demanded that I make the other boy stop looking at him. Instead, I advised Alonzo to get to work, in which case he would be too busy to worry about the other boy's looking at him.

Immediately Alonzo leaped up, shouting at me to do my job and take care of that other student.

Since this was early in the school year, the other students didn't yet know what to do about this sort of behavior, but they were beginning to grasp the concept of ownership of responsibility. They were watching the episode with interest.

I again told Alonzo to sit down and get to work, that the other boy was not the problem—that Alonzo had the problem. Alonzo loudly argued back that he didn't have a problem.

I asked the class who they thought had the problem, and they unanimously agreed it was Alonzo—that he was allowing somebody else's dirty looks to set him off and to give him an excuse to behave irresponsibly.

Alonzo began to shout at the class as well as at me. I told him to go to the time-out area until he could settle down and do his work. He refused.

I told him that in that case, he was out of control and I would take him to the Holding Area until he had thought over what he was going to do differently. He yelled that he wasn't going to the Holding Area either. I told him that he was, and escorted him out of the room. Before we could reach the Holding Area, however, he ran away from me and out of the building. I notified the principal that Alonzo was out of control and out of the building and that the institution staff should restrain him. They did so. Within ten minutes of his first day in my class, Alonzo found himself in an isolation room in the administration building.

On my first free period, I called the director of group life and asked him to meet me at the isolation room because I wanted to talk with Alonzo and wanted him as a witness. I added that I wanted to do the talking. He agreed.

In the isolation room, Alonzo tried immediately to talk about me and my problem—how I wasn't doing my job, how I didn't do anything about the other boy, how I let the other boy pick on Alonzo. I told him that my behavior was not debatable, that the only thing for discussion was how Alonzo was going to get himself under control—that he had been agitating from the start, that I had given him three alternatives, all of which he had rejected, that he had disrupted his own and his classmates' education, and that all that was unacceptable. I wanted to know what he planned to do differently. He stared back at me. I waited.

Finally, Alonzo muttered that if I let him come back to class, he would not do that anymore. I told him that if he came back to class there were some things I wanted him to make a commitment to do:

1. to be courteous to me and to his peers;
2. to do his work without argument (asking for help if he needed it);
3. to go to the time-out area if he began to think he couldn't do the first two; and
4. to ask me for some suggestions if the time-out wasn't enough.

Alonzo agreed to the terms, and returned to class, and abided by his commitment for a full two weeks before needing to be controlled again. Each time since then, his own control has lasted longer, and required briefer (though just as determined and consistent) control by others.

Teacher's Attitude

In gaining control, as in everything else you do, it is important to treat the student in a caring, concerned, and respectful way. Do not be overbearing about it. Arrogance and one-up-manship and NIGYYSOB ("Now I gotcha you son-of-bitch") games have no place in caring relationships, nor has revenge. Remember that you are gaining control because to allow a student to be out-of-control is to allow him to hurt himself and to steal his peers' education. You care too much about him and them to allow him to do that. You care too much about yourself, also, to have your right to teach frustrated. Furthermore, not to intervene is to communicate that the student is not worth helping or beyond help, and you have given up on him.

Thus, self-respect and respect for all the students is the motivating force behind your actions. Your actions and the attitude and manner with which you carry them out are the model for future student behavior. In watching you, they will be "psyching out" all the nuances, including your motivation. They will begin to imitate you. You want them to imitate your manner and attitude as well as your overt behavior.

Be flexible in applying the tools of control: do not overkill, but use enough force (physical or verbal) to be quickly effective. With experience you will become adept at choosing and applying the correct approach to a given situation.

Once you have chosen a course of action, *be firm*. Have the courage of your conviction. The right motivation and attitude will more than compensate for any error in choice of tool.

As with the physician, "above all do no harm." If you are motivated by caring and concern in gaining control, the result of your intervention, whatever it is, will be to help rather than to harm. These students are masters of detecting motivation; their radar systems are superb. They will know whether you are trying to embarrass them, put them down, get your kicks at their expense—or to help them.

Occasionally, a teacher whose overall motivation is OK loses it under extreme provocation. A teacher is not God. Extreme or prolonged stress can bring out anger and a desire for revenge. If that happens, and you punish or take revenge on a student, apologize to him as soon as you are aware of it. An apology is a sign of strength, not weakness, a sign of grace under pressure. It is an admission that you, like the student, are human and not infallible. By apologizing you are not only recapturing a proper attitude for your behavior, but also giving him a valuable demonstration, a model for appropriate behavior. (In apologizing, be assertive and direct, never fawning or obsequious. If your apology is not accepted, that is not your problem; drop it and go on with the business at hand.)

It is a good idea to check out your own attitude and communication style frequently, whenever you are engaged in controlling disruptive students. To do this, Transactional Analysis' Parent-Adult-Child communication model is useful.* In using control tools, your communication should be coming from your Rescuing Parent, Nurturing Parent, Leadership Parent, or your Adult ego states, and never from your Critical Parent, Persecuting Parent, or Child states.

Ask your friends to give you a "reading" now and then, if you are in doubt, about your communication and attitude. Sometimes our attitudes can deteriorate under the stress without our being aware of it.

To care about others, one must first care about self. Respect yourself, your needs, and shortcomings. As you check your attitude, notice if you are showing signs of stress—discouragement, cynicism, tiredness, loss of confidence, irritability, loss of feelings of accomplishment and self-worth. Are you wondering what you are doing here? Bored? Having trouble in your relationships with friends, family, colleagues? If so, take steps to do something about it. The last chapter, on burnout, gives some suggestions for taking care of yourself.

---

*See Transactional Analysis bibliography at the end of Chapter V.

Figure 1. Early Control Flow Chart (before Triads are functioning & caring milieu is strong).

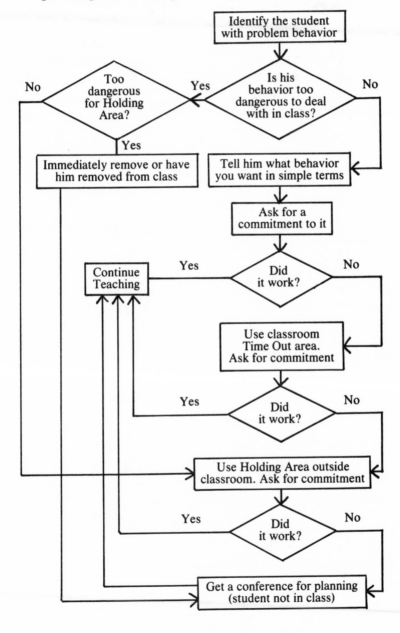

Suggested Readings

Bassin, Alexander, Bratter, Thomas E., and Rachin, Richard L. (eds.). *The Reality Therapy Reader.* New York: Harper and Row, 1976.

Glasser, William, M.D. *Reality Therapy*. New York: Harper and Row, 1965.

4. The Next Stage: Assessment and Establishing Triads

You, therefore, who teach another, do you not teach yourself?

Romans 2:21 (NAS)

Philosophy

William Glasser describes four behavior requirements for a healthy life: A person must learn how (1) to give and receive love, (2) to gain worth and recognition, (3) to have fun, and (4) to be self-disciplined.* Students with behavior disorders have become woefully deficient in their attempts to achieve these skills.

They are not concerned about each other, but only about themselves. They are egocentric, but not

---

*William Glasser, *Reality Therapy*, Harper & Row, New York, 1965; and *Positive Addiction*, Harper & Row, New York, 1976.

convinced of their self-worth or of their worth to others—and therefore they continually test adults, challenge authority, and either try to impress their peers, or withdraw altogether. Their "fun" is full of danger and anxiety, and consists either of tormenting others or of lonely activity. Self-discipline exists only in the most rudimentary form and only in the achievement of egocentric ends. They operate on the "Pleasure Principle", needing immediate gratification of needs and impulses and unable to wait for a distant payoff.

Thus, in a classroom of such students, the teacher is confronted with all these problems, en masse, and it is his sole responsibility to deal with them. He is bombarded with aggression, attempts by students to impress peers at his expense, by a host of unfulfilled needs clamoring for immediate relief, or by despair. It is no wonder teachers feel overwhelmed, sag under stress, "burn out," become angry and disillusioned, and/or leave the field.

No one teacher can cope with all this challenge or meet all these needs. Nor should he try. By doing all the giving, he deprives the students of the pleasure and opportunity of learning to give and care and help. He keeps them in the one-down position of always being the receiver, never the giver.

The approach described here, developing a "caring classroom," avoids the head-on challenge, but remedies the problems. It specifically creates a milieu, and a method of operation within which the students can be successful in meeting Glasser's classic four behavior requirements: They can care for others and be cared about in return; they can experience self-worth and recognition for healthy, appropriate behavior; they can develop inner controls; and they can have a good time doing it. And they do it themselves, in an atmosphere created by the teacher, with the teacher's support. The teacher doesn't do it for them—doesn't give all the love, caring, gratification, discipline, and fun.

To oversimplify vastly, this is accomplished by structuring the class into triads, groups of three (carefully selected) students who work together, and are responsible for each other's support and progress, caring and control. (There is precedent for this in Fader's concept of "students helping students,"* in which he uses triads as a tool for academic progress in learning to read, and also in "Positive Peer Culture,"** in which small groups are used for behavior control.)

The reader may wonder why triads are used— why not diads, or groups of four? After all, "three's a crowd."

Twosomes can be too intense, not allow for distance or dilution if a member needs time out, do not give the necessary amount of support, and can lend themselves to collusion in destructive or otherwise

---

*Daniel Fader, *The New Hooked on Books*, Berkeley Publishing Corp., New York, 1976.
**Harry H. Vorrath & Larry K. Brendtro, *Positive Peer Culture*, Aldine Publishing Co., Chicago, Illinois, 1974.

self-defeating behavior. If the two members are of equal strength, not enough strength can be brought to bear to influence change in one or the other. Likewise, a group of four can too easily become two groups of two, or contain too many combinations of possible interactions, becoming too complex and too stimulating—too complex in requiring too much help for too many people, becoming exhausting and not subject to control. It is too easy to hide or get lost in a group of four.

The triad is complex enough but not too complex. The idea is to "keep it simple," but not so simple it cannot work because of insufficient resources. For example, if one member of a triad is tempted to misbehave, two can stop him where one could not. If a member does not understand a problem, he has two teachers within the triad—and if one of them needs a time-out, he still has one helper left. If two members do not understand a problem, the one who does understand it can teach until either one or both of the others has grasped it, at which point he either has a helper for ongoing teaching of the subject, or all three can go on to another issue.

In the caring classroom, the triads are used for several things: for academic progress and support for self-control, caring external control if necessary, and also for providing consistent, *ongoing* overt commitment to help and care about one another—to give each other positive "strokes" and to protect each other from self-imposed harm. How this all happens will be described in detail as we go along.

First Day Explanations

On the very first day that I meet with a class, I tell them that this classroom is different from others that they have known: that here they will be expected to care about each other; that here we solve our own problems together, helping one another;* that we don't take our problems to the principal or others. I tell them that I am not a policeman and I won't get drawn into being one—I am a teacher and I won't be diverted from that. In no way am I going to let any one disrupt my teaching. I also tell them about the holding room and the time-out area and how they are used.

I then tell them that sometime next week I am going to sort them into groups of three who will work together from then on. Each student will be responsible for teaching as well as learning. Each student, with me, will be responsible for what is learned by the other members of his group who, in turn, will be responsible for what he learns.

---

*I also tell them that here they will be learning survival skills— how to get along in the world and be able to take care of themselves. I give them examples of how, if they don't know how to read or do basic math, they will be "taken," victimized by others, or be at the mercy of their own ignorance and resulting poor choices. I tell them how learning is power. The academic component of my class is weighted toward survival skills, toward consumer and legal and political education, and toward solidifying continuous basic knowledge. (See Academic Functioning of the Triads, p. 94, below.)

I tell them that if any member of the group has a problem, that problem will then belong to all three of them, and that they will be responsible for helping each other, with my supervision. Rather than talking with one person, I will be talking to the group; if I make a presentation of some academic material, it will be to the group, who will then be responsible for teaching each other. All problems arising within the group will be resolved within the group. Unless I say so, no group is to become involved with another group, either academically or in regard to behavior problems. If a member of a group needs to leave the room for any special event, for tutoring, or to go to the lavatory, the other two go with him.*

---

*I am describing my situation with my students when the triads are established. The expectation that the triad members accompany each other when outside the classroom may or may not bear modification, depending on the situation. For example, my students are all seriously behaviorally handicapped and need the support and restraint of their peers' presence, especially early in their experience. Once I know them better and they know each other better, this practice is modified. I and the peers may then decide that a student is able to leave the room unattended.

By the time a student is ready to move on to a regular classroom, he must be able to take responsibility for his behavior without his peers present. The needs and rights of each student for privacy and self-determination should be weighed with his needs for peer help. The type of classroom you have ("special" or "regular"), the type of setting, and the ability of your students to take responsibility for their own behavior will determine the need for the triad members to accompany each other. Students whose behavior is normal and dependable would probably never need to be accompanied by peers except when working together on a project.

When told this, they are intrigued, and don't know what to make of it. They usually ask for explanations and especially how I will choose the groups. I tell them that I will explain later if they are still interested, how I arrived at the groupings. I tell them that I will be spending this next week gathering all the information I can about them, and (like Fader*) I tell them that I will then process that information according to my own secret formula and come up with the groupings. (It is important that you maintain your conviction that this works and that they need not worry about it.)

Forming the Triads

Assessment. During the next week, the task is to gather as much information as possible about each student. The students spend the time taking standard math and reading diagnostic tests, and pursuing a variety of different activities designed to increase my understanding of them. Additional information is usually available from past records in the office.

I find that having each student give me a "journal" entry every day is a useful diagnostic tool. I give them the following list of topics to write about and ask them to select a different one each day.** (I give them no instruction on how *much* to write.)

---

*The New Hooked on Books, 1976, p. 13.
**Selected and adapted from Harvey Wiener's list in *Any Child Can Write,* McGraw-Hill, New York, 1978, pp. 226–227.

A time I felt happy
A time I felt proud
A time I was very sad
A time I was very scared
A time I was disappointed
An argument I had with a friend
A time someone helped me
The last time I helped someone
A time I got in trouble
My definition of happiness
My definition of fear
My definition of a friend
My definition of courage
My definition of caring

This list gives enough of a selection to give some idea of the student simply from what he chooses to write about—and does not choose. At the same time it is not so overwhelming as to be discouraging and confusing.

These journal entries not only give an idea of writing skill, but also a level of insight and coping skills and problem-solving, and of particular stumbling blocks and sensitive areas. This information is then factored in with the other data in forming the triads.

Case illustration: Mario chose to write about a time he got in trouble. In a brief essay he described how angry he had been when blacks began to move into his combative, ethnically-defensive Italian neighborhood. His resentment had been so violently expressed in school that he had been expelled repeatedly for fighting and finally sent to the institution. He concluded his journal entry this way: "I guess I'd better learn to live with it (racial integration) because they (blacks) are here, too. If they'll leave me alone I'll leave them alone."

Data:
- Mario has a problem with race.
- He has begun to recognize a need to change the way he deals with it (less violence, ignore them)
- It is important that Mario learn how to relate to black people as human beings; it is not good for him to stop at his mutual-non-interference accommodation.

Plan: Place him, if possible, in a triad with one black member who is unlikely to react violently to his racism. (Note: Placement with two black students would be too threatening to his controls.)

At first Mario tried hard to ignore his black partner, working parallel to him but not with him. I talked with the triad about the importance of helping each other, and gave them assignments and projects in which they had to work together. By the end of the year Mario was at ease with both members of the triad and they had become friends. He was then mainstreamed back to the school in which he had gotten into trouble (which was frequently in the headlines because of outbreaks of racial violence).

I was worried about how Mario would fare when he returned home. I feared that his gains were too fragile and that the peer pressure from his old friends, to hate and fight blacks, might push him back to his former ways. One day I shared my worries with a black colleague of mine; she replied that she had a good friend (also black) on the faculty of Mario's school who might be willing to take a special interest in him. I called her friend and told her about Mario and she said she would be glad to help him.

Subsequently this teacher reached out to Mario in a very supportive way. She told him that Mr. Carducci was very interested in him and his progress and had called her to tell her about him. She encouraged him to let her know if she could be of any help. When she saw him in the halls she asked how things were going, and one day when he seemed under strain she took him aside to talk. Gradually Mario opened up to her and began seeking her out for understanding, advice, and encouragement. She has kept me informed from time-to-time, and Mario has been able to stay in school and out of trouble, and, equally important, has made two friends whom he would formerly have seen as enemies, either to be fought or avoided and ignored.

That teacher is, of course, now a resource when other students leave my class for that school. It is through such serendipidy that networks can be built.

Speaking of serendipidy, there is a significant role for it in devising the triads. It would perhaps be reassuring if I could give you an easy mathematical formula for weighting data to form the triads. However, I do not have one. I use a lot of empathy and intuition, based on knowledge and experience, and there is really no substitute for that. I talk with each student and make crazy little notes on things I notice, with ideas about what group each might fit into. Sometimes it is a toss-up—and sometimes those toss-ups result in your best triads.

When, after all this, you have managed to form the triads so that they are working the way you want them to, serving their purpose, it is wise, if possible, not to tamper with success. Therefore, if a student leaves and creates a space in a triad, as new students are assigned to my class, I look for his "twin" to fill the vacancy.

Also during this first week, I give each of the students a copy of the "Problem List" from *Positive Peer Culture** and tell them to choose some other or others to help them memorize it. Who each student chooses provides more data for forming the triads.

Generally, this week is one of low pressure, relaxation, and getting acquainted. The teacher does a great deal of talking with individual students about the test results. I make up a work folder for each student, individually geared to his needs as I learn about them from the diagnostic tests, and maintain this individual folder throughout the school year.**

Selection of the Triads. At the end of the first week you will have enough data to form the class into triads. Here is how you can go about it. Sit down in quiet and solitude with all your data and begin to rate the students, according to ability to give both academic help and support for coping behavior. Your strongest, most adequate student is at the top of the list, the weakest, least adequate is at the bottom. Give greater weight to ability to give academic help than to ability to give emotional support.

---

*Reproduced at the end of the chapter.

**This folder contains the material the student is focussing on at any given time. For example, if a student is having difficulty subtracting numbers containing a lot of zeros, I will make up a sheet of special problems for him to practice. I may write the student notes about other books and materials I want him to use, and these assignments will be put into his folder.

Although you will have a lot of data, you will still have to make some arbitrary judgments and will probably make some errors. Don't worry about it, you can correct them later.

After you have ranked all the students, divide the list from top to bottom in three equal parts, the top third, middle third, and bottom third. Place these three lists side by side. Form the first triad by taking the top name from each list. Form the second by taking the second name from each list. And so on until all the names have been used. Each triad now has a relatively highly functioning member, a relatively low-functioning member, and one somewhere in between the other two.

To put this another way, suppose you have 15 students in your class: rank them from 1 to 15, 1 being the highest functioning and 15 being the lowest functioning, according to your criteria and data. When you divide this list into three parts, the first list will contain names 1 through 5, the second list names 6 through 10, and the third list names 11 through 15. The first triad would be made up of students 1, 6, and 11. The second triad would be made up of students 2, 7, and 12, and so on until you have five triads.

If your class is not evenly divisable by three, you may have one or two groups with a membership of two students. In other words, if you have one student left over, take a member of one of the triads to work with him, thus giving you two groups of two students. If you have two students left over, they become one group with only two members.

You may find later that some of the triads are seriously mismatched. For example you may find that you have put together two aggressive students who have been carrying on a long bitter feud. Although eventually you want them to be able to deal with their feud, the intensity of the feud may be so great, and their inability to deal with it now so acute that it is sabotaging your immediate goal, which is to create triads in which students can begin to work together. You may therefore need to make some changes in the composition of some triads, as you learn more about your students.

Once you have determined the membership of the triads, you announce them to the class and have them begin working together. What you have created is a classroom full of assistant teachers, whom you will now supervise. Eventually all the students will act as teachers, helping you. One specific important benefit of this is that you have made it possible to share the helping-teaching role. Any student who teaches or helps another is demonstrating to himself and others his worth and his adequacy. He is learning to care by practicing caring.

The Triads and Systems Theory

A system is a whole made up of related parts. For instance, a mobile is a system: if you tap one part, the whole begins to move and rotate. A family is also a system, of members who relate to each other in certain ways according to certain roles. If one family member stops performing his role, the whole family is affected and other members begin changing the way they operate and relate to each other.

Likewise, a classroom is a system made up of students and teacher, who interrelate with each other and with the rest of the school (which is a still greater system of which each classroom system is a member). If one member of a system changes, the whole system is changed. If one member of a classroom changes, the whole class is changed.

By changing the way he relates to the class, the teacher has changed the character of the class, and it then has to make adjustments accordingly. If the teacher sees the class as one large amorphous mass, and acts toward it as if it were, the class will tend to respond as a mass.

By breaking it up into smaller parts, the teacher has changed the entire character of the system. Each triad has become a mini-system, made up of its three members plus the teacher. Because the teacher is a member of each triad, the teacher is the common binding element, like the wires for a mobile. The teacher, therefore, has increased his influence on the system, while decreasing the influence of any one student on it.

By breaking up the large system into smaller discrete ones, the teacher has made it much more difficult, if not impossible, for a strong aggressive or passive-aggressive negative leader to become a change agent for the entire system. He will have only two followers rather than the entire class. It is no longer a case of the embattled teacher facing a single large mass of hostile students. You are in control, and you can relate to small manageable units rather than to one unmanageable mob.

You also have put them in an unfamiliar situation. They aren't sure what to expect, and are more hesitant to challenge you on your own turf. Their old roles may not work any more. Some leaders will prefer to wait for awhile to size up the situation. By then, it will be too late, because you will already have had time to begin the therapeutic work of the triads. For those who don't wait to challenge, you have your tools ready, and the followers are not readily available—again, because they are divided into small units, and because they are even less sure of themselves than usual in the unfamiliar situation.

Thus, the teacher who finds himself anxious about a class of potential hostile challengers, revolt leaders, and underminers, is now in a much more comfortable and secure position. It is no longer a "me against them" scenario. Furthermore, instead of having the responsibility to teach and change each student individually, the teacher, by treating the class as a system of mini-systems, has become much more efficient.

Now when teaching to one member of each triad,* the teacher has set up a condition whereby

---

*By "teaching to one member" I mean that although all are participating, the teacher makes sure that at least one of them is clear about the content at every step and can teach it to the others. The teacher monitors this process and teaches how to "tutor."

the other two members of the triad have to respond
to that member, rather than all three responding to
the teacher. The teacher acts, and then reverbera-
tions of change travel through the system, each element having an effect on each other one. The
teacher is required to expend much less energy,
while the students share the expenditure of energy
in the positive direction in which the teacher has
moved.

Academic Functioning of the Triads: Students Teaching Students

The academic functioning of the triads is very serious and important business, especially for students
with behavior disorders. While the atmosphere of a
caring classroom is typically that of joy and relaxation, it must not be forgotten that survival is at
stake. I sometimes tell my students that "surgery is
taking place here"—to emphasize that we are all engaged in vital activity. I challenge the students right
away by telling them that in this class they are going
to be treated with respect, and given difficult work
to do and difficult problems to grapple with, and that
because it is so difficult everyone's help will be
needed.

A Core of Shared Material. For students to be able
to help and teach each other, it is necessary that
they have a core of materials that they are all familiar with or working from. One can easily see how

discouraging, scattered, and out-of-control the situation would quickly become if the classroom were a smorgasbord of exotic (albeit attractive and fascinating and seductive) materials from which students could pick or teacher assign at random. A student cannot help his peer if the peer is struggling with something with which the prospective helper has no familiarity.

Therefore, you will find it invaluable to have in your classroom a collection of automated materials, programmed to an ascending order of difficulty and complexity, in which each level depends on mastery of the previous level. An example (by no means the only one) of such materials is the SRA math and language packages. The teacher may prefer materials of his own design or adaptation, to use either as the base of or as a supplement to purchased materials. I use purchased materials supplemented by my own in several patterns.

For example, I have written my own social studies course which all my students use, each student progressing at his own rate and supplementing with non-programmed assignments and projects of individual interest and need. Conversely, I have designed my own approach to grammar and reading, which is supplemented by purchased programmed materials, all of which are used by all the students, again each at his own pace. I use still a third variation for math, using purchased programmed kits as the base, supplemented by programmed mastery tests and problem worksheets of my own design—all of which are used by all students.

The important point is to have programmed materials that form a shared common foundation for the triad, but to which students and teacher are not limited. The teacher must be free, as a creative professional, to improve upon, supplement, or substitute materials to help his students learn.

You can use the programmed materials as a diagnostic tool in assessing the level of mastery of each new student. Then he and you both know what level he has reached in terms of being able to help others. When all the students work from the same core of materials, every member of each triad knows where he is and where each of his peers is in relation to the shared materials.

I may deviate from the materials by suggesting other special projects related to the core (for remediation of a special problem, for example). In such an instance, the other members of the triad are listening while I am suggesting and explaining—so they understand the instructions and can help if needed.

One programmed commercial computational math kit* begins with whole numbers, and addition, subtraction, multiplication, and division of whole numbers, fractions, decimals, and percents. A diagnostic kit pinpoints problems by means of a survey test and diagnostic worksheet. This process lends itself to the remediation of the math problems most of these students will be developing or will have developed. Peers in the triad who have mastered the material are expected to help students working on material at the lower level.

---

*There are several good ones on the market.

I have also developed math mastery tests which are not provided by the purchased core itself. For example, as a student completes a computational skill, I begin talking with him about *applying* his skill to word problems. I will tell him, "you may know *how* to multiply (or divide), but you need to know *when* to do it." I then give him word-problem worksheets (of ascending levels of difficulty), which I have designed so he can begin to master the practical application of the basic math skills. (Soon I will often hear this student explaining this to his peer in exactly the same way, and even with the same intonation—which demonstrates how well he has understood not only the content but also the manner in which it has been presented).

The Process. One characteristic of these students that is striking, in addition to their emotional immaturity and impulsiveness, is that they are generally unable to approach problem-solving (social or mathematical) in a logical, thoughtful, practical, systematic way. They tend to give up easily at early frustration, with no tools to overcome it. Here is where the sympathetic helping peer is terribly important.

It is not at all unusual in a caring classroom to hear a student, who has begun to master the basic computational skills and problem-solving process, begin to mimic you by saying to his frustrated peer, "I know it's tough—I had the same problem. But now I can do it, and if I can, you can too. Let me help you." The teacher, then, is able to reinforce that helping attitude by praising the helper. He can also reinforce the struggling student by telling him how glad he is to see the student beginning to deal with a frustrating problem.

97

Early in the basic mathematics mastery, and early in the development of the caring classroom, it is important not to overwhelm the student. Keep it simple. He is fragile, and his peers are not certain of the helping role. However, by the time the student has mastered the most basic material and is beginning to go on to deal with a higher level skill, he is familiar with the problem-solving approach to application of his skills, and is also familiar with the helping process. At this point neither teacher nor peers need to be so "gentle" with him. They can now begin to make more demands on him (always in a caring and respectful way, of course).

The idea is to foster the development of relationships in which the student becomes strong enough as a person, through the relationship, to make it possible to demand greatness and maturity from him and put more responsibilities on him. Thus he grows in both knowledge and emotional maturity simultaneously.

Values and the Process of Mastery Learning. The reader may have already identified the above with Bloom's "Mastery Learning."* Mastery learning is especially important for insecure students who have often had the scary feeling of not having mastery over themselves, their behavior and feelings, or of anything else in their lives. Much of their intolerable

---

*Benjamin S. Bloom, *All Our Children Learning, A Primer for Parents, Teachers, and Other Educators*. New York: McGraw-Hill Book Co., 1981.

behavior is an attempt (gone astray) to wrest some mastery from a totally chaotic environment.

Bloom has said that he does not believe mastery learning is appropriate for the severely disturbed or violent student. I disagree heartily. Mastery learning fits in beautifully with the whole philosophy of the caring classroom. But, it must not be simply the promulgation of one lone value, namely academic security. Mastery learning must be supported by the caring milieu. In the caring classroom we want the student to learn the values of helping and accepting help, and that in the process of helping another one establishes proof of his own worth as a person. *At the same time* he learns to value and develop academic and problem-solving skills that will serve him all his life.

Some may think that the very fact that students are mastering *something* (e.g., an academic skill) will automatically change their behavior and values for the better. It does not happen that way. To the contrary, they may become smug, arrogant, exclusive, manipulative, all at the expense of others, using their newfound skills to overpower others, put others down, and ridicule them.

The reader will recognize that the approach of demanding mastery of difficult subject matter is totally opposite from the popular approach in which the teacher gives the delinquent a pleasant task and then rewards him for doing the task. For example, here the teacher does not "seduce" the student to learn by giving him a book on auto mechanics, because he happens to love auto mechanics; rather, in the caring classroom the teacher tells the students that certain difficult things will be expected of them, and that they will be challenged to give of themselves helping others to learn difficult material that is important for them to know.

The "seductive" approach tends quickly to become over-stimulating, scattered, lacking in substance, and accompaned by high anxiety, as students become less and less certain of where they are in the material, what they have actually accomplished, and where they are going. The student (for example) may have read a book on auto mechanics, and his peer may have read a book of poems. But how does this relate to their academic problems and goals? And how do they relate to each other? How have their values and behavior been changed by their experience? Chances are neither they nor their teacher know!

In other words, the student who reads the book on auto mechanics should be reading it not because it's fun or interesting, but because it will address something he needs in his educational progress. Likewise, the poetry reading should be related to a diagnosed need that the teacher, the poetry reader, and the other members of his triad are aware that he has. The education of these students is serious business and their time and effort needs to go into mastery, according to a careful plan.

To put it another way, in the caring classroom reinforcement comes from the sense of self worth that comes with triumphing over problems, mastering tough material, and most of all giving and receiving in a caring reciprocal relationship in which one gives as much as he gets.

More Details on the Process. Let us look in more detail at how the triads function academically. What has been said above is applicable to all subjects. In teaching English, I may make a presentation on sentence structure (e.g., What is a sentence?) to the entire class. I then ask everyone in the class to write out an example of a sentence. I go to each triad to check the work. If one student in a given triad has it right and can explain it to me, it is now *his* job to help the other two in his triad to understand the work. If two understand it, they teach the third. I then move on to the next triad, and so forth.

If at least one member of each triad understands the presentation, I now have at least one-third of the class as assistants. Nobody in my class is getting lost, I am expending much less energy, and am sharing the satisfaction. Nor do I need to feel guilty about the quality of the teaching.

Most teachers have had the experience of being frustrated after many unsuccessful attempts to explain a concept to a student and to have another student say, "I think I know what he's having trouble with. Let me run it down for him." Frequently peers can be better teachers than the teacher because they are so close to each other's situation. The teacher can be so familiar with the material that he has long since lost his understanding of where the difficulties are in grasping it. Schools where it is used, find that student tutoring of other students works very well.

If there is a triad in which nobody understands the concept, I work with that group, but focusing my effort on the member who is closest to grasping it. Meanwhile I am modeling helping behavior and teaching technique. As soon as one student in that group understands the work and can explain it to me, I can now tell him that it is his responsibility to make sure his partners understand it and can do it.

Sometimes there will be a triad which has a student who has good math skills but no student with good language skills. It is then my responsibility to move into that triad and fill the gap until one member has learned sufficient language skills to be able to help the other two. Later, I can occasionally circulate back to the triad, checking to see that the process is working.

Depending on the level of work being done by each triad, you may decide to give a presentation to the entire class (if everybody or almost everybody can benefit from it, or is at about the same level on the subject I am presenting). Or you may opt to make a presentation to one triad, or several triads together. Always teach to the most capable student, making sure that at least one member of each triad understands and can explain your presentation. Then let them teach while you oversee, supervise, make suggestions.

The member of the triad who is least capable academically also has ample opportunity to give help: He has his input and works in tandem with the others, often making practical or creative suggestions. Sometimes this member has special kinds of insights even though he is academically behind. He may also quiz the more advanced students in spelling or math drills. The most capable student receives his compensation, for his time and effort helping his peers, in the form of more individual time and attention and special tutoring from the teacher.

No longer can a student ignore his peer. If a member of his triad does not understand the work, a student can no longer say, "That's none of my business." His success depends on the success of the entire triad. His responsibility is focused and limited. He does not have to care about or give help to his entire class—which would be overwhelming (and can court grandiosity). He is only responsible to help and be concerned about the other two members of his group, as they are with him.

Before concluding the discussion of the academic functioning of the triads, I want to stress the enormous importance of survival skills for youth suffering from behavioral problems. For obvious reasons, these children are usually dismally retarded in their acquisition of basic skills. This, combined with their poverty of inter-personal skills, places them at huge disadvantage for survival in society.

While you are helping them to grow affectively (which we shall discuss in the next chapter), it is absolutely essential that your academic focus stress the basic skills necessary for independent living in the community. These basic skills include functional adequacy in the legal, political, and consumer spheres. In addition to such obvious things as ability to read a newspaper, calculate discounts, figure the cost of materials to make repairs on living quarters, figure a tip, write a coherent business letter, fill out a job application, and balance a checkbook, these youngsters need to know about getting legal consultation, political advocacy, discharging the responsibilities of voting, and consumer protection. They need to know what their rights are and specifically how to exercise them.

These children, inadequate today in school performance and affective functioning, are at grave risk of becoming "the inadequate adults of tomorrow,"[*] unable to manage their personal finances, unaware of their rights, not knowing where to turn for help.

They will become engrossed in learning these survival skills once they see the very real benefits they can provide. There is power in self-sufficiency and independence, in not being somebody else's "sitting duck," "sucker," or victim. In my class, we talk about the need for being a shrewd shopper in the face of sales competition, about planned obsolescence. I challenge them to identify the best buys among the sales ads, and to figure out how much they save by careful shopping. We role play going to a bank, taking out a loan, and figuring out what the payments will be. We identify their ward aldermen, public committee members, and councilmen, and discuss how they obtain office and what their duties

---

[*]Norman Tutt, *Care or Custody*. New York: Agathon Press, 1975.

are. We interview them in regard to specific concerns.

I do not mean in any way to discount the joys of reading fine literature for recreation, the delights of pure math, or the expressive pleasure of creative writing (there are opportunities for these), but the reality is that such satisfactions may have to wait for many of these children, if indeed, they discover them at all. Meanwhile, they must survive.

A Note on the Questions Parents May Have. Within our society generally, and within specific groups, and within individuals, the competing values of personal achievement and cooperation often coexist in uneasy and unstable truce. Sometimes we wish to excel over our peers, to attain individual fame and acclaim regardless, and sometimes to be grandly autonomous—in spite of the feelings or the needs of others. At other times we want to be popular and an accepted part of the group, enjoying the submerging of self in the whole—warmly sharing. Often we want both to be the Lone Hero and The Good Team Player. Schools have often intensified this conflict.

Parents sometimes find themselves caught in this dilemma: They want their children to be happy and popular, but at the same time they want them to progress academically as quickly as possible, and not be held back by others. They may want their children to be the "best student." This is a very uncomfortable yet common conflict, given the competing and complex values of our world.

The great strength of the caring classroom model is that it presents students and parents with a way out of the dilemma. It is no longer an "either-or" situation, but an "and-and" situation. Each student progresses as fast and as far as his individual ability will allow, and at the same time he is able to be a giving, caring member of the group, which in turn cares about and gives to him.

Psychologists have long known that active learning is far superior to passive learning, and that teaching is one of the most active means of learning. Studies have shown that when students tutor other students, all of them benefit and improve significantly, but the tutors learn and progress even more dramatically than those receiving the tutoring. And the progress is not only in the cognitive sphere, but also in the areas of social skills, self-esteem and confidence.

Parents of the students who are more academically skilled may be worried that the time their youngster is spending helping his peers is holding him back from progressing more rapidly. They can be reassured that such activity is actually strengthening the academic excellence, progress, and achievement of their children.*

Parents may also be concerned about the company their children keep (i.e., their peers in the

---

*For a dramatic example of such parental concern followed by relief and reassurance, see *Children Teaching Children,* Op.Cit, p. 69.

triad). This is an intelligent concern. Usually in society generally, the "good" child does not lift his "bad" associates' behavior up to his level; rather, the good behavior often deteriorates to that of the more irresponsible members of a peer group. "Bad company corrupts good morals," as the saying goes.

In the case of the caring classroom, however, the teacher is constantly insisting on, modeling, teaching, coaching, and reinforcing good behavior. Good behavior becomes the norm. It is not left to chance or uninterrupted peer influence. In the case of this model, the parents need not fear their children's company.

Much has been said in recent years about the importance of the school in developing the moral character as well as the mind. One thing is certain. It is not by preaching moral homilies or by giving little lessons in ethics that moral character is formed. The moral sense develops under the discipline and examples that define desirable behavior. This must be supported by stern measures to check or prevent misconduct.*

It is critical that the teacher make every effort to be available to the parents to discuss their children's experiences in the classroom and the philosophy and methods you are using; just like the administrator, they are part of the team. Parents should be encouraged to visit and even drop in to the classroom without appointment as soon as visiting is possible.

---

*Paideia, Op.Cit., p. 55–56.

Problem Solving List

1. *Low Opinion of Self Problem:* Often feels put down or of little worth. When solved: Is self-confident and cannot easily be made to feel small or inferior. Is able to solve his problems and make positive contributions to others. Doesn't feel sorry for self even though he may have shortcomings. Believes he is good enough to be accepted by anybody.
2. *Inconsiderate of Others:* Does things that are damaging to others. When solved: Shows concern for others even if he does not like them or know them well. Tries to help people with problems rather than hurt them or put them down.
3. *Inconsiderate of Self:* Does things that are damaging to self. When solved: Shows concern for self, tries to correct mistakes and improve self. Understands limitations and is willing to discuss problems. Doesn't hurt or put down self.
4. *Authority Problem:* Does not want to be managed by anyone. When solved: Shows ability to get along with those in authority. Is able to accept advice and direction from others. Does not try to take advantage of authority figures even if they can be manipulated.
5. *Misleads Others:* Draws others into negative behavior. When solved: Shows responsibility for the effect of his behavior on others who follow him. Does not lead others into negative behavior. Shows concern and helps rather than taking advantage of others.
6. *Easily Misled:* Is drawn into negative behavior by others. When solved: Seeks out friends who care enough about him not to hurt him. Doesn't blindly follow others to buy friendship. Is strong enough to stand up for himself and make his own decisions. Doesn't let anyone misuse him.
7. *Aggravates Others:* Treats people in negative, hostile ways. When solved: Gets along with others. Does not need to get attention by irritating or annoying others. Gets no enjoyment from hurting or harrassing people. Respects others enough not to embarrass, provoke, or bully them.
8. *Easily Angered:* Is often irritated or provoked or has tantrums. When solved: Is not easily frustrated. Knows how to control and channel anger, not letting it control him. Understands the putdown process and has no need to respond to

challenges. Can tolerate criticism or even negative behavior from others.

9. *Stealing:* Takes things that belong to others. When solved: Sees stealing as hurting another person. Has no need to be sneaky or to prove himself by stealing. Knows appropriate ways of getting things he wants. Would not stoop to stealing even if he could get away with it.

10. *Alcohol or Drug Problem:* Misuses substances that could hurt self. When solved: Feels good about self and wouldn't hurt self. Does not need to be high to have friends or enjoy life. Can face his problems without a crutch. Shows concern for others who are hurting themselves by abusing alcohol or drugs.

11. *Lying:* Cannot be trusted to tell the truth. When solved: Is concerned that others trust him. Has strength to face mistakes and failures without trying to cover up. Does not need to lie to impress others. Tells it like it is.

12. *Fronting:* Puts on an act rather than being real. When solved: Is comfortable with people and doesn't have to keep trying to prove himself. Has no need to act superior, con people, or play the showoff role. Is not afraid of showing his true feelings to others.

From *Positive Peer Culture* by Harry Vorrath & Larry Brendtro Aldine Publishing Co., 529 South Wabash Ave., Chicago, Ill. 60605

Suggested Readings

Adler, Mortimer J. *The Paideia Proposal, An Educational Manifesto.* New York: MacMillan, 1982. See especially pp. 16–18, on survival skills.

Alper, Michael. "All Our Children *Can* Learn," *University of Chicago Magazine,* Summer, 1982, Vol. 74, No. 4.
On Mastery Learning.

Bloom, Benjamin S. *All Our Children Learning, A Primer for Parents, Teachers, and Other Educators.* New York: McGraw-Hill, 1981.
On Mastery Learning.

Brandt, Anthony. "The Schools Where Everyone Gets A's," *Family Circle Magazine,* 3/17/81.
On Mastery Learning.

Fader, Daniel. *The New Hooked on Books.* New York: Berkley, 1976.

Gartner, Alan, Kohler, Mary, and Riessman, Frank. *Children Teach Children, Learning by Teaching.* New York: Harper and Row, 1971.

Strain, Phillip S. (ed.). *The Utilization of Classroom Peers as Behavior Change Agents.* New York: Plenum Press, 1981.

Tutt, Norman. *Care or Custody.* New York: Agathon Press, 1975.

5. Affective Functioning of the Triads

Affective Education—A Definition: *Generally speaking, affective education concerns emotional development. As such, it includes the educational efforts related to attitudes, values, and feelings. There are affective components related to the self (self-concept and self-esteem, for example), social components in relationship to other human beings (empathy, justice, various social values, acceptance of special children), and to objects (love of literature or nature).*

William C. Morse, et al
*Affective Education for Special Children and Youth**

---

*Published by the Council for Exceptional Children, Reston, VA., 1980.

*I*t is important to emphasize that affective and cognitive education are inextricably bound up together. Teachers fool themselves if they think they can ignore one in favor of the other, because human beings simultaniously think, feel, and act. In this book, when we speak of affective *or* cognitive education, it must be understood that the division is artificial, for the purpose of focus.

Why Affective Education?

Dr. James P. Comer, Director of the Yale Child Study Center Schools Program, writes:*

A school that is able to address student needs in an orderly way—*first* with attention to social and psychological comfort and trust and *then* through academic and intellectual growth—is in the best position to prepare students for successful living in the complex society of today and tomorrow. (italics ours)

The Issue of the "Pleasure Principle" and the "Reality Principle." Students with behavior disorders have not developed emotionally from a very immature level. They are stuck. One useful definition of immaturity, which well-describes these students, is that it is a state of functioning on the "Pleasure Principle";** there is a need for immediate gratification,

---

*In *School Power,* Free Press, New York, 1980.
**See Bruno Bettelheim's chapter on "Education and the Reality Principle," in *Surviving, and other Essays, Op.Cit.*

an inability to postpone pleasure for greater pleasure or gratification later. Conversely, maturity is a state of being able to function on the "Reality Principle": there is an ability to endure a certain amount of frustration, and wait for greater pleasure and satisfaction later.

In the normal course of growing up, we all start out operating on the pleasure principle, and gradually develop the ability to operate on the reality principle. The transition takes place with the support of a helping, caring relationship with parents, and consistent experiences of finding that gratification and satisfaction eventually do come to us.

For example, a newborn infant, wanting dinner, will cry persistently until it comes. No matter that mother is busy with something else at the moment or the bottle isn't ready. No "explanation" will satisfy—only dinner! Only now! The toddler in the high chair, however, having had the experience over and over that mother eventually does bring dinner, and now seeing mother in the preparations for dinner, will wait patiently and cheerfully, trusting in the expectation that dinner will be forthcoming in awhile, and that the hunger pangs will be assuaged. He can do this partly because trust in eventual gratification has been built up through repeated gratifying experiences, and partly because he loves his mother and pleases her by waiting patiently without having a tantrum.

On the other hand, a child whose experiences have taught him that food may *not* always be counted on, that it may be insufficient or sometimes not forthcoming at all, and who can't rely on his mother to meet his needs, will learn two things: (1) I must rely on myself, and I can't trust the future; and (2) I can trust only in the food I can see *right now* and can hold in my hand *right now*.

The problem with such learning is two-fold: (a) the child cannot truly rely on himself to meet his own needs because he doesn't have the resources, and (b) most of life (the real state of affairs) is characterized by the need to wait. The piano player drudges through hours of practicing scales and exercises before reaping the satisfaction of mastery and recognition. The employee waits for paychecks and promotions. The mother endures nine months of the discomfort of pregnancy and then the hard labor of childbirth for the final satisfaction of having the child. The potential home buyer works and saves until he has a down-payment and qualifies for a loan.

Most people get enough immediate satisfaction during the waiting/postponing process by thinking about the distant payoff which will make the present state of frustration all worthwhile. But not the immature person who is operating on the pleasure principle. He will feel miserable to the point of not being able to wait. He doesn't trust that the final payoff will ever come for him. He doesn't believe in the future, only in the present—only in the bird (or the food or the car) in the hand. Only so long as he is getting satisfaction *right now* can he be happy. And since he can't endure any current unhappiness, because it may never change, he settles for whatever satisfaction he can get at the moment.

Thus, we find the immature person stealing the car he can't save for; and we find many people succumbing to the lure of the credit card, and bankrupting themselves in their desire to have all the things they want *right now*.

The significance of all of this for education is that education itself is based on the reality principle. The student drudging through memorizing his multiplication tables is doing it primarily not because it is fun, but because his teacher and parents say it's important for his future, and he trusts and wants to please them. The pilot-to-be slogs through seemingly endless hours of studying textbooks and working math problems, while his friends are out having a good time, not because the studying is more fun than being with his friends, but because he dreams of the day when he will solo and believes that that future thrill will make all the studying worthwhile.

The mature student eventually will study on his own, without the teacher or parent forcing him, because he has come to internalize the belief that the present drudgery will pay off in the end; that the mastery will come and bring its own satisfaction; that he will earn a diploma and that will lead to other satisfactions; that he will solve this problem and it will eventually lead to his solving big problems that will bring big benefits.

Education is a process in which the learner gradually takes over more and more responsibility for his own learning. He learns to think and solve problems, and ask new questions that lead to another aspect of his inquiry, and enable him to solve and master more and more of it. He is able to become creative and independent, and no longer has to have his teacher standing over him defining the problem and reinforcing the assignment, having to be told what to do and when to do it.

The immature person stays at this dependent state and is therefore never truly educated. On his own, without his teacher, he is at sea. And the reason for such a sad state of affairs is not because of intellectual limitations, but because of emotional, or affective limitations. To overcome this problem therefore, teachers must take into account the affective state of the child.

Needed: A Workable Approach to the Issue. I have found affective education, through the use of the triads, to be the matrix within which cognitive academic education can take place. It works. It takes into account where the students are now (generally immature) starts there and works toward growth and maturity. Appropriate support and gratification take place in the relationships that develop within the triad, including the relationship with the teaching adult. Thus, the student experiences a realistic, supportive, and helping relationship with an adult and with his peers, and learns to cope with the problems that arise in these relationships. The experiences in the triad move the students along the continuum from the Pleasure Principle to the Reality Principle. Let's see how this happens.

Problems as Opportunities. There is one thing we know about these students—Sooner or later, usually sooner, a problem will arise. There are two ways a teacher can react to a problem: (a) with dread, and efforts to avoid it or get rid of it; or (b) with a welcoming attitude, viewing it as an opportunity to teach coping, to remedy the difficulties on which these kids are foundering.

People who respond to problems in the first way are prone to become "Rescuers," a harmful, destructive role about which more will be said below (p. 148). Strenuously seek to overcome any tendency you have to view problems with dread. Seek to develop a tendency to take a positive attitude toward problems as opportunities. On your success in this will depend your ability to help your students.

If you find you have some difficulty with this, it may be very helpful to find a "coach," who can help your growth in being able to handle problems. Especially study and practice assertiveness. Assertiveness and "Rescuing" cannot co-exist in the same person at the same time. (See p. 122 below, for more on assertiveness).

Problem-Solving in the Triad

Let us imagine that a student comes to class very upset and begins to thrash around and challenge you. This, you have evidence to believe, is his usual behavior when he thinks things are going wrong in his life. He doesn't know what other behavior choices are available to him; or he may have a vague idea, but despairs of being able to follow through on other choices. Now, fortunately for him and for you, you have an opportunity to change that.

As always, the first item on the agenda is to box him in so he makes a commitment; only now when the triads have been formed, the commitment is made between him and the members of his triad, and the teacher. The members of his group are partners in supporting his keeping his commitment.

"Checking."* One of the tools the peers use in helping a partner maintain a commitment is "checking." By "checking," they are calling attention to unacceptable behavior, behavior that he has made a commitment not to use (in this case, the impulsive, hyperactive thrashing around and challenging). To identify unacceptable behavior, they use the *Positive Peer Culture* "Problem List" that you have asked them to memorize. In this case, the student is showing evidence of the problem called "aggravating others."

He may also have an "easily angered" problem, but that is not clear yet. Don't discount his right to be angry. He may have a very good reason to be angry, which may not yet be clear to you. What he *does* with his anger is the issue.

When they see a lapse into this behavior, the peers will tell him to "check" himself—meaning,

---

*See Vorrath and Brendtro, *Positive Peer Culture*, Op.Cit.

"Stop and notice what you are doing." But how they do it is important. The teacher must model, explain the need for, and insure kindness and caring in the manner that checking is done. It is always to be done in a helpful way, with a helpful motive. It is not to be used as a means of playing "I gotcha."* It is not a put-down or a discount, or a way of humiliating someone. It is, instead, imparting useful information: "I want you to notice and do something about behavior that is hurting you." "I care about you and don't want you to go on hurting yourself."

When one peer "checks" another (by saying, "check it"), checking is an external control. After awhile, however, students will begin to "check" themselves, without being told to. You will notice, and they will report, that they are checking themselves before anyone else does, or when no partner is around. At that point, checking has been incorporated as an internal control. Internal control is self-control, a necessary step to maturity and health.

While the partners in one triad are dealing with the problem, with your assistance, demonstrations, and supervision, the rest of the class continues to work. However, what is happening in that triad is not lost on them. They are quietly and subliminally taking it all in. In some respects, although you have not announced it or interrupted work for conscious observation, you have created a "fishbowl," in

---

*One of the "games" identified in Transactional Analysis, often known as "NIGYSOB": "Now I Gotcha You Son-of-a-Bitch!"

which one group learns by acting while the others watch and learn from the watching.

The rest of the class never participates unless the teacher asks them to. (An example would be when one student is so out-of-control that his triad cannot control him, and the teacher believes more peer help is needed. The message in such an instance is: "You are not so out-of-control that 14 peers cannot help you. You are not stronger than the class. We will not let you hurt yourself this way.")

When a triad is working with one of its members on his keeping his commitment, you may hear dialogue like this: "What's the matter, man, can't you control it? We can help you deal with it later, but right now you're stealing my education . . . Maybe you'd better go to the time-out area for awhile so we can get on with it." After the student returns from the time-out area, he talks with his triad about his commitment to change (with the teacher present so he can hear it too, as a member of the support system). (Note: As yet there has been no discussion of alternatives—only of the need to stop the unacceptable behavior).

Reversal and Re-framing. Usually, because this is one of the most striking characteristics of these students, there will be great resistance to the commitment (although not as great when dealing with peers as when making a commitment to an authority figure). The resistance will often appear in the form of a projection of blame onto somebody else: "How can you expect me not to act that way? He was bugging me!"

This is a perfect opportunity to use two tools, called "reversal" and "re-framing." The "reversal" is a placing of responsibility back on the person who is manifesting the unacceptable behavior, getting him to own his own problem. He wants to put the responsibility for his behavior onto somebody else, implying that the other person has to change first. To be allowed to insist on this is probably never to change, however, because one can only change oneself, not others. One can assist another to change himself, but cannot actually change another. Thus, to think another is the cause of one's own behavior is an irrational thought, and not to be encouraged.

In order to reverse the responsibility back onto the student who owns the problem, one uses the related techniques of "re-framing" (or "re-labeling")—actually redefining what the student has said. In this example, in which the student blames his own bad behavior, on another student's "bugging," the teacher would re-frame the situation thus:

T: "What you're saying is that he has a problem?"
S: "Damn right!"
T: "Are you saying that when people have problems they should be punished?" (If the student had done something to hurt the person who "bugged" him) or
"Are you saying that when somebody else has a problem it's OK for you to hurt yourself?" (If the student's bad behavior was self-destructive—as with a tantrum) or
"Are you saying that when somebody gives you a problem the best thing to do is to run away from it?" (If

the student's behavior has been to leave the room or cut class or otherwise avoid responsibility)

In other words, create a conflict in the student by focusing back on the problem of his own behavior and the incongruity of his rationalization. This is the beginning of his becoming involved. You are asking him to make a value judgment—something many of these students have seldom thought about.

Values Clarification and Assertiveness Training.
Everyone has values. Values are what we want, think, and believe, the basis for how we behave. Problem students often behave impulsively and have never stopped to think first about the beliefs their behavior springs from. Even some passive students, who are not particularly impulsive, base their behavior almost completely on their feelings, and only dimly perceive the beliefs whence their behavior originated.

All troubled students are hampered by a poverty of values choices, that results in a poverty of behavior choices. Rigid and impoverished, they cannot appreciate values different from their own, yet have never carefully looked at their own to see if they stand up to the light of examination.

If one is to change his behavior, one must change the values the behavior is based on. Sometimes values change first, followed by behavior change. Sometimes behavior changes first, followed by a reassessment of what one believes. Sometimes the process is so ongoing that it is difficult to determine what changed first. What is certain is that these students need to reassess their values, change their values, and change their behavior, and the process is all of a piece.

New values and new behavior choices need to be offered to the students to replace their impoverished ones. One means of imparting new values is to model them, and the teacher has ample opportunity to do that. If the teacher is potent, and the students like and admire him, they will begin to try on his values and behavior.

However, modeling alone is usually not enough. Yours is constantly undermined by the many other very different models the students see: the alcoholic father, the neglecting mother—or vice versa—the hostile teacher, the drug pusher, the "slick operator," the bully, the two-faced ingratiator, etc. Something is needed to make values clarification and the relationship between values and behavior more powerful and clear. Assertiveness training is an excellent means of doing just that. Experiential learning is combined with didactics in a here-and-now practical way that enables the student to get in touch with values, and to translate them into behavior that gives him immediate positive feedback.

Assertiveness training is "the study and practice of appropriate, responsible, comfortable behavior which stands up for one's own rights while fully respecting the rights of others."* It has been widely

---

*D. J. Carducci, "Positive Peer Culture and Assertiveness Training: Complementary Modalities for Dealing with Disturbed and Disturbing Adolescents in the Classroom," *Behavioral Disorders,* May, 1980.

written about in the past decade as a powerful treatment and socializing tool, especially useful for groups characterized by feelings of powerlessness or beset by aggressive impulses. However, although disturbed students (and sometimes their teachers) represent just such a group, for some reason assertiveness training has not been generally recognized and adopted as a useful tool for dealing with classroom disruption. I am at a loss to understand why this is, as I have found this approach of huge benefit to my students, and to me as well in dealing with them.

Some people are reluctant to consider assertiveness training as an option because of a lack of understanding about what assertiveness is.

Because we tend to value interpersonal conflict negatively, people are concerned lest our newly assertive clients go about the land picking fights, tilting at windmills, and generally stirring up trouble . . . this because assertion has been confused with aggression. The difference is easy to see, (because) assertions respect the rights of others, and assertive behavior treats others with dignity, while aggression violates the rights of others, and is self-aggrandizing at the expense of other people. . . . We must ask whether it is appropriate to counsel passivity in the face of injustice or aggression from others, given that passivity takes its toll in decreased self-respect, increased defensiveness, and, often, brooding resentments which fuel further conflict at a later time.

Assertive responses thus fall between passive response or nonresponse, on the one hand, and aggressive overresponse on the other. Both extremes have negative consequences assiduously to be avoided.* In addition, assertive behavior does itself have positive consequences which, once having been identified and experienced, are potent sources of incentive and motivation for future appropriate problem solving. Subjectively, newly assertive people report 'feeling good' about themselves and their behavior, *whether or not* the specific outcome of their assertiveness is totally successful.**

By practicing the assertiveness tools (which are, by the way, easily taught and easily understood and used), students learn appropriate new behavior, which is dramatically different from their old offensive and inadequate behavior, yet enormously satisfying. These assertive responses include, at appropriate times, such things as the nondefensive admission of problems, the expression or acknowledgment of risky feelings such as anger or sadness, the presence of "soft" feelings such as caring and loving, and the expression and clarification of wants and thoughts, desires and requests, and beliefs.

When one finds himself in an uncomfortable situation, and faces the old dilema of "flight or fight," assertiveness provides a third and healthy choice. Our aggressive students have learned to fight to get

---

*In TA terms, Aggression is "I'm Ok, you're not OK"; passivity is "I'm not OK, you're OK"; and assertiveness is "I'm OK, You're OK."

**Robert Erikson, Ph.D., and Judith Carducci, RCSW, CAC, "Assertiveness Training Interventions and the Alcoholic Family System," paper given at the National Forum of the National Council on Alcoholism, Washington, D.C., April, 1979.

their needs met, our passive students have learned to flee, and the passive-aggressive have combined both by fleeing to fight underground; but nobody has taught them how to be appropriately, responsibly assertive. They are behaviorally deficient, not because they can't learn, but because they haven't been taught. They need to be taught.

So far here, we have not dealt with how to help a student select the way he is going to behave instead, if he is not going to continue with his prior unacceptable choice of behavior. To ask a student to stop doing something, but not help him find a better alternative, is a very unfriendly way to treat him.

Case illustration:* A student in one class was repeatedly being "set up" by a slick, manipulative classmate, but the rest of the class and the teacher did not see what the tormentor was doing; they only saw the end result, which occurred when the victim had had all he could take and blew up. The class had identified the victim's problem (from the Positive Peer Culture "Problem List"**) as "easily angered," and whenever he exploded, they would tell him to "check it." The student became more and more upset: Not knowing how to deal appropriately with his tormentor, he had been suppressing his feelings, exerting control over them as long as he could. When he couldn't hold them back any longer, the "checking" by his peers implied failure, and threw him back again on the only so-

---

*From Carducci, in *Behavior Disorders, loc. cit.*
**See pp. 89 and 108, above. Make sure your class has memorized this list so they can identify problem behavior. As pointed out earlier, this form of labeling is a way of simplifying concepts and helping students "own" the problem they need to change.

lution he could think of—more suppression. Thus, the student found himself in a vicious circle in which he was becoming increasingly frustrated.

Finally, the student blurted out what the other student was doing to him, but that information was met immediately by a "reversal":

"You mean he's got a problem. Isn't it interesting how you're dealing with it?"

Student (to teacher, in angry frustration): "What should I do about it then?"

Teacher: "You think about it."

Student (in complete frustration): "Shit! If you don't know, how do you expect me to?"

Result: The tools of "checking" and "reversal", unaccompanied by any discussion of acceptable alternatives, resulted only in incomplete control and only escalated the student's frustration, striking another blow at his already poor self-image. The suppression he chooses is not a comfortable alternative, but merely another form of "flight" or avoidance of a real problem. The problem does not get resolved, and the person suffers from still more discomfort from trying to sit on his clamoring feelings.

Assertiveness skills fill this need. In this case, a "DESC script" might have been useful. In a DESC script,* one Describes the situation, Expresses what he thinks or feels about it, Specifies what he wants, and states the Consequences (pro or con) that will result.

Here, the student in distress could have said directly to the manipulator:

---

*See S. A. Bower and G. H. Bower, *Asserting Yourself* (Phillipines: Addison-Wesley, 1976) for a fuller presentation of this tool.

(D) "You have been messin' over me for a long time, like stapling my folder together just now.

(E) "When you do that, I get mad as hell. It really gets to me, man. It interferes with my work and my concentration.

(S) "From now on, I want you to leave me and my work alone; tend to your own business and let me tend to mine.

(C) "If you do that, you and I will both get our work done. If you don't, I'm going to ask the teacher for some help in getting you off my back."

Another example of a DESC script in the same situation, if the student is not yet assertive enough and confident enough to deal directly with the instigator:

(D) (To teacher) "I'm having a problem. Leon is doing a lot of things to bug me. He needles me constantly. Just now he stapled my folder together.

(E) "I'm afraid I'm going to blow up and get myself in trouble. I don't know how to deal with it.

(S) "I want to talk over what I can do besides getting in a fight with him.

(C) "If I can find some way of getting him off my back, I won't get in trouble and I'll get my work done."

At this point, the teacher and the student do some classic problem-solving (see next section).

These examples may sound sophisticated, but they are the natural result of your having taught them how to do this, and role-playing and modeling, and practice.

Once the student has had help from the teacher and the members of his triad, he may feel confident enough to say to the manipulator, in a caring way:

(D) (None)
(E) "I think that your 'aggravating others' is going to get you in a lot of trouble.
(C) "I know some dudes who would bust your head open if you ever pulled the same crap on them. I'd hate to see that happen to you.
(S) "I think it would be a good idea for you to talk with your group (triad) and Mr.——, about what's going on with you and what you can do differently.
(C) "If you do, I think you could get it together and you'd feel a lot better about yourself."

Note the values that are implicit in this script: That one has a right to say what he wants, thinks, and feels; that he has a right to decide whether or not he will become involved in another's problem; that one cannot change another but can change how he deals with him; that solving a problem is better than living with it; that getting oneself in trouble because of what another does is not a good way to deal with the problem; that one need not suffer alone—others can help if they choose to; that one can ask for help without losing face or dignity.

By acting in a way consistent with these values, the student begins to incorporate them in his regular behavior. They become further clarified for him when he, in practicing assertiveness, has to stop and get in touch with what he wants, thinks, and feels, in order to express himself and specify the solution for which he hopes to obtain cooperation.

With practice, the students will deal with situations calling for assertiveness themselves, within the triad.

Case illustration:* Tyrone, a 15-year-old black youth from the inner city, needed a novel to read in class, and asked permission to go to the library. As was customary, he was accompanied by the other two members of his triad. He asked the middle-aged, middle-class, white female librarian if she had a book entitled, "The Autobiography of a Pimp." She immediately became angry. Hostile words were exchanged, ending with Tyrone's exclaiming, "Fuck your damn library!" and storming out. His peers were able, using the control tools, to get him to calm down and return to the classroom. When they arrived, Tyrone was muttering angrily and his peers were talking earnestly to him in low tones. They retired to the "time-out" area to confer without disturbing the rest of the class, and I joined them there.

Tyrone figured that the librarian had taken his request as a "put down" because of the word "pimp." He decided she probably thought he was trying to be "smart-ass" and to give her some trouble. However, he didn't know what to do. A review of assertiveness tools followed, and Tyrone and his peers decided that a "DESC script" was appropriate. He would return to the library, Describe the situation—namely that he had asked for a book he had read at his former school and that she, possibly misreading his intent, had become angry; Express his feelings—that he had not intended any disrespect or trouble; Specify what he wanted—to have an understanding with the librarian so that (Consequences) they wouldn't feel hasseled by each other, he could ask for books comfortably and she would not be angry.

Tyrone role-played this script with his group until he said he felt comfortable with it. Several changes were made in the wording, and he was coached on his tone of voice, eye contact, and body language. When he was

---

*This case is also described in Carducci, *Ibid.*

ready, the trio returned to the library, where Tyrone went up the librarian, hung his head, and murmured, "I'm sorry," and left.

His peers brought him back to the "time-out" area where they pointed out to him that he had not been assertive at all. They asked him what had happened (he had panicked into "flight" when out of the "safe" role-play situation in the classroom). Discussion ensued of his fears about the possible consequences to him of both aggressive and submissive behavior (a values clarification exercise), his legitimate rights, the librarian's legitimate rights, and his catastrophizing (a tendency which interferes with assertiveness), and whether or not it was realistic. More role-playing was practiced. Eventually, Tyrone went back to the librarian.

They still do not understand each other well—the differences between them are wide, and although Tyrone is actually a sensitive boy, willing now to meet people more than half way, the librarian is a closed, tense, rather narrow-minded person, fending off what she perceives as a threatening world full of frightening youths. While Tyrone is open to change, she is not. Tyrone, however, has learned a very valuable lesson: You cannot change another person (only the other person can change himself and only if he—in this case she—is willing), but you can change how you deal with her.

Assertiveness and Black Students (and other minorities)—An Added Dimension

In the case illustration of Tyrone, I noted that the black teenager and the white middle-aged librarian will probably never understand each-other. Under any circumstances it is difficult enough for two different generations to understand each other; here the factor of racial-cultural differences compounds the problem. More needs to be said about assertiveness and racial-cultural differences.

People often remark about my lack of problems in my interaction with black students, and I have given some thought to why that is so. I believe my ease with black students is a result of a combination of long familiarity and intimacy with blacks, respect for their culture and experience (familiarity does not breed contempt), and lack of defensiveness on my part about our differences and who I am.

I grew up in a small coalmining town, where my family and our black neighbors were similarly poor, oppressed by the mine management, and tormented by the Ku Klux Klan. As a teenager and young man I was the drummer in a black jazz group whose leader was my best friend. Later I worked with street gangs, living in a black neighborhood. Thus, my growing-up experiences were entwined with or closely paralleled those of poor socially-depressed black youth. In some ways it is easier for me to empathize with them than with middleclass or privileged white youth. Black language and communication styles are not foreign and frightening to me. The word "mothafucka" doesn't shock me. I don't find my black students a threat.

In this respect I am more fortunate than most of my white colleagues. Many whites do not understand the different implications of words in the two cultures*. For example, "pimp" has very different emotional impact on the librarian than it does on Tyrone and his peers. Conversely, the word "boy" has opposite emotional impact. Whites may misunderstand the black game of "playing the dozens"** as dangerous aggression and become intimidated.

Nevertheless, whites who do not have the advantage I have had can develop an understanding of and respect for the feelings and communication style of their black students if they (1) are secure enough not to be defensive, and cultivate an "I'm OK-You're OK" attitude of self-respect and respect for others, (2) are open to being taught by blacks about their language, style, feelings, and experiences, and (3) once recognizing the differences, respect them. This takes some work and some time and can be quite a challenge, but is essential for establishing an integrated caring classroom.

This same educational process is necessary for teaching assertiveness to black students. Situations which for whites are simply a matter of having one's dignity at stake, for blacks may be fraught with dan-

---

*By limiting this discussion on "two cultures" (one black, one white), we are oversimplifying for focus and emphasis. There are, of course, many varieties of black culture, just as there are of white. We are here ignoring the cultures of the rural south and the "assimilated" black middle class, among others, to focus on that of the urban, underprivileged delinquent "street" youth who are most likely to be embroiled in "culture shock" with their white teachers. Tyrone is an example.

**A game of verbal one-up-manship which, characteristically, calls the reputation of the players' mothers into question.

ger. What is assertiveness in a black-black interaction may be misunderstood as aggression by whites.

Assertiveness is an important survival skill for black students, but learning it must involve also learning that appropriate assertive behavior in the black community can be very different from what is considered appropriate behavior in the white culture. So teaching assertiveness to black students means in effect teaching them a foreign language at the same time they are being taught a survival skill. It does not ask them to lose their black communication style, but rather to be able to communicate appropriately in *both* cultures.*

The principles of openness to and recognition of cultural and ethnic differences are applicable in teaching students of any minority, e.g. hispanics, orientals, American Indians, etc. Females in our society face special assertiveness problems also, and there are a number of books dealing with assertiveness for women. It behooves the teacher to be familiar with the special implications of assertiveness for young women.

In order to teach assertiveness, it is important that the teacher himself be appropriately assertive, in order to be an effective and believable role model both outside and inside of class. As a general rule, teachers of assertiveness should possess the following characteristics: empathy and respect for others,

---

*To understand this in depth, the reader is referred to the book *Assertive Black . . . Puzzled White,* by Donald K. Cheek, Ph.D. San Luis Obispo, CA: IMPACT, 1976.

genuineness, concreteness, ability to confront and be direct, openness, immediacy (ability to act in the here-and-now), and self-actualization (having developed in oneself the qualities he wants to teach— behaving consistently with what one teaches). If possible, enroll in an assertiveness training course and get coaching. Read several books on assertiveness and practice what you read.*

Classic Problem Solving

Student: "I'm mad as hell at him! I'm really pissed off!"

Teacher: "I know. You have a right to be angry. What I'm concerned about is what you're *doing* with your anger. It's OK to be angry, but what you *do* about it may or may not be OK.

"You have choices about what you do. *How do you decide?* Let's talk about it, OK?"

How the decision is made (about how to deal with the problem producing the anger) is based on problem-solving skills. People may solve problems all their lives without ever stopping to think about how they do it. This is both good and bad: good, in that if we always were self-conscious about the process we would not be able to make decisions in the clutch and would slow ourselves down just when speed is needed; bad, in that we frequently garble the proc-

---

*See bibliography at the end of this chapter for some that are excellent.

ess, skipping important steps or tripping on dangerous terrain, or make decisions too quickly and sloppily when care, precision and deliberation are needed.

Troubled students are prone to go from need or impulse directly into action, altogether skipping the problem-solving step, or—in the case of the conniving game-player—choosing a faulty solution, and skipping the step of considering the relative merits of consequences.

The teacher of troubled students has a responsibility to teach classic problem-solving, as an essential element in caring about one's self and others. The following is a useful model.

Step 1. Define the problem. Is it really one problem or is it a bundle of problems all mixed up together? (Remember the WW II soldier at K. P.? He had to extricate his one potato from all the others before he could begin to work on it.) There is little so discouraging as not knowing what is wrong or where the punches are coming from, nor more overwhelming than thinking that "everything" is going wrong. Talk it over with others. Get their help in sorting out one problem from another.

Step 2. Once the problem is defined, Brainstorm Solutions. This is a step on which many people have trouble. Watch out! To brainstorm is to let one's imagination run wild. Many people stop themselves from doing this in one of two ways: either they don't believe they have choices, or they immediately think of all the negative aspects of a solution, and in the process discard it. Let us look at each of these separately.

Do we have choices? As a matter of fact, there is no problem under the sun for which we have no choice as to what we can do about it. We even have choices about what we can do about death and taxes! We can accept approaching death with an attitude of serenity or with bitterness or denial; we can hasten it or postpone it to some extent; we can take our own life or leave the time of our departure to God. Similarly, we can pay our taxes, be honest or cheat, or withhold them altogether in protest, and go to jail for our beliefs; we can put part of them in escrow and embark on a long legal maneuver. Etc., etc.

The dead-end we tend to drive ourselves into is confusing "no choice" with "no perfect solution." Perfect solutions are seldom to be found in this world. Poor choices abound. What we usually have in life is a bunch of poor choices; but be grateful— that is better than no choice at all. I can think of nothing more hopeless than a conviction that I have no choices about what I can do. That is to be truly in despair. However, to believe that is to play a dirty trick on oneself, because while cognition exists, choice exists.

Premature assessment of the solutions: Since we have only imperfect solutions, we can also drive ourselves to depression by immediately discarding *any* possible solution, because it is faulty, and then concluding that we have no solutions.

In brainstorming, then, get as many heads together as are willing to work with you, and write down every solution that comes to mind, no matter how zany. One crazy idea will often have a friendly way of triggering a dandy, which would have remained boxed up in your collective brains if you hadn't first opened the way with its improbable predecessor. (Your students will be both astounded and delighted by the variety of possibilities that will be suggested. Soon, their natural creativity will take over, and they will come up with ideas that will boggle their minds.)

Step 3. Assess the Consequences. Here is an activity that is new to aggressive students, who tend to act without regard to the consequences or ethical implications of their behavior. Some of the weirdest solutions will be discarded immediately as too bizarre to be considered. Others will be examined thoughtfully, with attention to both pros and cons, and with careful regard to legal and ethical, and emotional or physical consequences. Even so, the number of workable choices will be a surprise to the students, who have had no idea of the richness of behavior choices available to them.

Step 4. Pick the Best One—even though it is not perfect.

Step 5. Do it. Put your plan into action. It won't work so long as it just stays an idea on paper. Adopt it as your own.

Figure 2. Problem-Solving Flow Chart

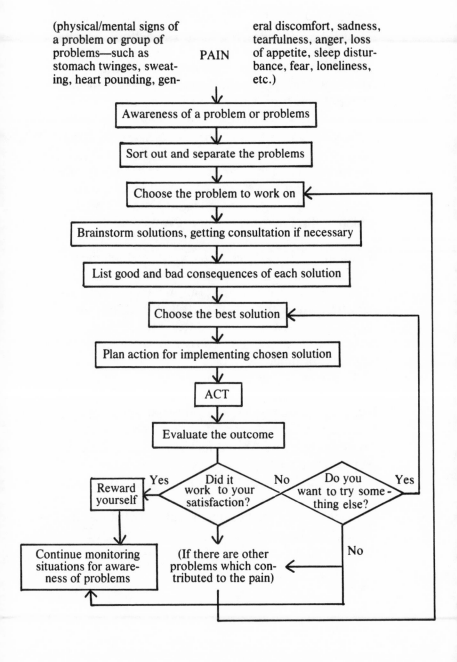

Step 6. Evaluate the Results—did it work? Can you live with the results? What did you learn from this? If you are reasonably satisfied with the outcome, you can give yourself a pat on the back (and accept pats from your peers), and you are now stronger and readier to take on the next problem.

Go over and over this process with the students until they have mastered it and can apply it in all situations, with individual and group, and both affective and cognitive problems. You have given them a tool for becoming adequate and independent which will serve them all their lives.

Maintaining a Versatile Tool Chest. No one theory, approach, modality, or tool is a panacea. A pen and an ax are both useful tools, but one won't do in a situation where the other is needed. Students are different and situations are different, so you don't want your flexibility limited by too restricted a selection of tools.

A narrow or parochial view is not helpful in teaching these students. I practice a thoughtful eclecticism, as can be seen. That is not to say that I recommend a reckless relativism and promiscuity. There are some ideas and methods that I totally reject as being hurting and irresponsible.

All tools that I use have certain qualities in common: They preserve the dignity and autonomy of the individual, they are not manipulative or mind-controlling, nor are they hurting or infantilizing. They allow respect for the learner. They further the

140

growth and eventual independence of the learner. (I see myself as a person who does things with, rather than to others.)

With these common evaluative factors in mind, I am constantly on a hunt for new and better tools, always trying to use an old tool in a better way, or to invent a new tool for a need for which I have no tool.

My recommendation is that teachers read regularly. If you don't subscribe to the professional journals, read them in the library. Read the reviews of new books, and read the books that promise to offer something new and interesting. Reread the old classics. If you don't have material readily available, see if your school can subscribe to a variety of journals.

Do not limit yourself to material from the field of education. Many of the most important influences on my thinking have come from other professions, such as social work, psychiatry, and medicine. Professional journals in the field of education can tend toward sterile "ivory-tower" intellectualism, or doctoral-thesis statistical stuff that is all but unusable by the front-line practitioner. However, even in these one can occasionally find an unexpected gem, or an impetus to a new idea or a fresh approach. Evaluate to be sure it fits into your value system and is not a complicating and de-railing anachronism. If it fits, integrate it!

Once you have seen a new tool and decided to use it, get as much supervised practice as possible. You will be clumsy at first, but that is not the fault of the tool. With practice, you will master it and will be looking for still another addition to your repertoire.

"Fronting." Suddenly you start to hear yourself being mimicked. The students begin doing what they have seen you model, saying what they have heard you say. They will even use the same inflection and body language you use. They try out the new behaviors much as an actor tries out a new role. They will even pretend to care and be helpful, even though they don't yet feel that way.

At that point, you fade back, and let them do as much as they can. Let them take risks. The term for what they are doing—*fronting*—may seem phony, and they may fumble around with it at first. But it really isn't phony, only new and unfamiliar. It's like learning to play the scale on the piano—halting and clumsy at first, but soon easier and more comfortable. Only after much practice will the new way of behaving cease to be a "front" and start to become real, an integrated part of the character.

Don't be concerned about fronting. Be glad the student is practicing acceptable behavior, perhaps for the first time. Encourage him.

However, you want to make sure your students do not remain at this superficial level of behaving. If not challenged, this new behavior will remain cosmetic, easy to accept as the real thing but not the real thing. Keep up a tension; we build muscles by having to use them, and new behavior becomes part of the character by being practiced—a lot. Give them *many* problems to solve. Do not let them rest on their laurels. Surprise them. When the classroom atmosphere begins to look too placid, throw a monkey wrench into it. Give them a new challenge and force them to face it, to make choices, to solve problems time and time again.

If I feel that all the triads are working very smoothly and a comfortable routine has settled upon us, I may suddenly make an uncomfortable change.

For example: The triads have had the privilege of going to the library without first asking me for permission. A triad has simply taken a red piece of wood (which identifies them to a hall monitor as being from my class) from its hook near the door, and gone quietly on their way. Suddenly I announce that they may no longer do that; that the entire class will go to the library together and only at a specified time.

The first time I do something like this, there is an immediate uproar. They want to know why—did somebody screw up? No, I just decided to do it this way. Loud protests follow, that I am unfair, it's a bad rap, that "this is just like all the other rotten schools I've gone to, man!" Someone is sure to lose his cool, get up in my face shouting and cursing and calling me everything in the book.

This is my cue to do a reversal—if I decide to handle the situation myself on a one-to-one with the rest of the class watching. "So, you say I have a problem; isn't it interesting how you're handling it? You'll find lots of things in life unfair. Does that mean you have to blow up and act irresponsibly about it?"

I may ask for comments and suggestions from the rest of the class, about how the student is behaving. Or, alternatively, I may simply refer the whole situation to the triads (if they are advanced enough) to deal with among themselves. After they have become able to cope with the

143

problem (usually in about a week or so), I will restore the original privilege.

By the time a student gets so wise that he knows I am using a tactic rather than just being nasty, and simply responds with a knowing smile to my machinations, he is about ready to move on. By then I am giving him his last intensive training to ready him for the realities of life outside my classroom. (See Chapter VII).

Don't let your students become comfortable with surface or primitive-level coping. It won't last or serve them for very long after they leave you. Your classroom is the "boot camp" for their life, the training ground. If they don't learn the survival skills they will need in life (academic and affective) from you, they may not have another chance. The morbidity rate of such children is very high. They tend to be the future dropouts of society, the welfare recipients, the jobless, the residents of prisons and hospitals, the alcohol and drug abusers.

Some Final Thoughts on the Affective Functioning of the Triads

The triad is a true group, and it is helpful to consider what that means from a theoretical point of view.

Experts in the field of group work have distinguished a number of curative factors inherent in the therapeutic group process. The importance of these factors varies, depending on the size, composition, goals, and types of groups, but *all* factors have been found to operate in *all* groups and to be interdependent.*

1. *The Imparting of Information*—This includes advice, suggestions, options, direct guidance about life's problems and/or didactic instructions given by the group leader or members.
2. *Instillation of Hope*—Hope is a necessary ingredient for this type of student—hope that things will get better, that they can learn, that rewards will come, that they can count on the future. Seeing their peers in various stages of progress instills hope: Those just beginning gain from seeing others like them who are "better" (more accomplished, less upset). Those further along can look at those just beginning and see how far they have come, and see their own progress.
3. *Universality*—This means the realization that one's problem or situation is not unique to him. (I am not all alone, different from everyone else; others have been here too.)
4. *Altruism*—Beginners in the group usually suffer from low self-esteem and hopelessness, feeling they have nothing to offer others. They are wrapped up in themselves. It is esteem-boosting to find that they are important to another and can help another.

---

*See I. D. Yalom, *The Theory and Practice of Group Psychotherapy,* (New York: Basic Books, 1975), "Curative Factors—Overview," pp. 70–103.

5. *Corrective Recapitulation of the Primary Family Group*—Teachers are often seen in the same authoritative position as parents, and peers are seen as siblings. The group, with its intimacy, offers a good opportunity to correct maladaptive ways of relating to primary authority (parent) or peer (sibling) figures.

6. *Development of Socializing Techniques*—Here we see social learning, or the development of basic social skills—how to deal with people in authority, how not to seem arrogant, or how to initiate an intimate relationship.

7. *Imitative Behavior*—Because of the opportunity to develop high levels of trust between group members, individual members can feel free to model themselves upon characteristics of others in the group. They may discover that some styles or behaviors are not appropriate or comfortable, whereas others are. Even where one adopted aspect doesn't wear well, the mere fact of taking the risk of trying something new will lessen rigidity, and make other risks easier.

8. *Interpersonal Learning*—This involves how to contract transactions between people.

9. *Group Cohesiveness*—The group is a haven, a safe harbor from life, a source of strength, of time-out, of mutual support, of a feeling of belonging.

   Signs that group cohesiveness exists will be:

   a. *enhanced communication among members:* In the early stages, most comments and questions will be directed towards the teacher. Later, communication will flow freely from member to member.

b. *high levels of trust:* Members will share more freely things about themselves that they are not proud of.

c. *assumption of group norms:* In the beginning, the teacher has to take responsibility for being sure members adhere to group norms. As the group becomes cohesive, the members themselves will check aberrations from the norm.

d. *development of ownership:* Members come to think of the group as *theirs.* Statements begin to contain words like "ours," "we," "us."

e. *Stabilization of roles:* Members show the true self more and more consistently, with less unstable "fronting."

10. *Catharsis* (ventilation of feelings)—It is axiomatic that the expression of strong held-in feelings is helpful in growth. Imagine the relief that comes from talking about anger instead of hitting or acting it out. Owning one's painful (hitherto thought to be "bad") feelings, and then being able to do something constructive about them, gives one true power and prevents the feelings from being crippling.

11. *Existential factors, including:*
    a. Recognizing that life is at times (often!) un-

       fair, but that it doesn't have to be a catas-
       trophe,

  b. Recognizing that there is no escape from
       some of life's pain—to live is to feel pain,

  c. Recognizing that no matter how close one
       gets to others he still faces life alone,

  d. Learning that each of us must take final re-
       sponsibility for our behavior, no matter how
       much guidance and support we get from
       others.

From the discussion so far, it can be seen that the triads provide all these curative factors with significant potency. By giving the students to each other in this way, and structuring their opportunities to deal with each other within such a therapeutic context, you are distilling and magnifying the healing experience, giving them a unique opportunity for learning and growth.

Beware of Rescuers and Triangles!

The Role of Pain in Change. "What could possibly be wrong with rescuing?" you may ask. "Isn't rescuing a good, kind, humanitarian way to behave? Shouldn't one always try to alleviate pain in one's fellow man?"

As to whether or not rescuing is good and kind and humanitarian, the answer is, "that depends." As to whether one should always try to alleviate or diminish pain, the answer is, "No—frequently not!"

To understand these answers, it is necessary to understand the role of pain.*

In his book *Anatomy of an Illness,*** Norman Cousins writes of the destructiveness caused by the *lack* of pain in leprosy (Hansen's Disease). Pain serves a useful purpose: It is a warning to the sufferer that something is going drastically wrong. In leprosy, the nerves are damaged by the disease process with the result that injuries or infections are not noticed (because no pain is felt), and this is why fingers, toes, and noses are lost. Sometimes, in physically exposed societies, toes are eaten off during the night by rats while the ill person, unaware because untroubled by pain, sleeps on.

So it is with psychological pain: The painful feelings are a signal that something is going wrong—an important need is going unmet. (This was described earlier, p. in the Introduction.) Pain, therefore, is to be respected and paid attention to. It should not be silenced with palliatives, without an effort to deal with the source, unless absolutely nothing can be done about the cause. To ignore a developing physical infection while blotting out the pain with painkillers is foolhardy, if not fatal. Likewise, some (many!) people blot out psychological pain with Valium or alcohol, while the cause goes ignored, until life is totally out of control.

---

*See Allen Wheelis, M.D., *How People Change* (New York: Harper and Row, 1970), chapter entitled "Suffering," pp. 1–8.
**New York: W. W. Norton & Co., 1979. See chapter 4, "Pain Is Not the Ultimate Enemy."

When a person is doing something self-destructive (which includes doing things that are destructive to others), or doing something ineffective in a crisis situation, he will feel pain, and it is that pain that will alert him that he has a problem. Without the pain, he will go on doing self-destructive, destructive of others, or ineffective things without knowing that he's in trouble until it is too late.

Pain, therefore, is a motivator for change. So long as I feel comfortable with what I am doing, I will go on doing the same things. Why should I stop, or change? If, on the other hand, I begin feeling some pain, I will start to do things differently.

What I do differently will depend on my perception of the source of pain. Being able to identify correctly the cause of the pain is extremely important for a successful result. If the source of the pain is really inside *me,* but I choose to believe that it is coming from *you,* I will do things that won't work. For example, if my behavior is such that people don't want to be friends with me, but I think the problem is that others are simply unfriendly, I will continue on a long fruitless search for friends, probably finally giving up in loneliness and despair because I have never been able to find the "right kind of person to be my friend." Some poor souls try "the geographical cure," changing their locale in an effort to solve a problem that is actually inside themselves, and thereby carry it with them to a new situation.

Even if the source of my pain actually is outside myself, coming from another person who is inflicting it on me, I probably can not change the other person (unless I want to use brute force, bullets, knife, electric shock, etc.). Since the only person I can ever count on changing is me, myself, I had better figure out what *I* can do differently about what the other person is doing to me. In other words, I must take responsibility for myself and my own feelings. (Here, assertiveness is essential.)

To put it succinctly: Comfort perpetuates the status quo. We all put great effort in maintaining homeostasis and resisting change. When the status quo is destructive, pain enters, destroying the comfort, and giving the important information that SOMETHING NEEDS TO CHANGE. The next step is to identify the cause or source of the pain, and then to discover and consider alternative courses of action which will restore comfort.

Figure 3.

The teacher's role is to assist the student in
(1) recognizing the pain (rather than denying or ignoring it), (2) identifying correctly the source or
cause of the pain, not projecting it onto others (if it
needs to be owned), (3) providing information on
workable alternatives, and (4) supporting the student
as he puts his chosen alternative into action and
evaluates the results. (See Classic Problem-Solving,
above, p. 135.)

There are times when you will have a student who
will behave abominably and yet will have no concern or anxiety about his behavior. It is everybody
else's fault, and everybody else be damned. He will
do as he pleases and the fact that his behavior is
causing others pain is "tough shit." In such a case,
the absence of pain (for him) is similar to the absence of pain in a leper. Ultimately it will be fatal for
him: He will end up alone, or in jail, or dead from
someone's revenge.

The obvious need is to do something so that *he
feels pain* as a direct result of his own behavior.
(See sections on control and commitment, p. 58.)
Box him in until he can't avoid it anymore, feels
pain, and has to focus on its source. Without feeling
pain, and connecting it vividly and inescapably with
the source (his own behavior), he will have no interest in changing.

What does all this have to do with rescuing? Rescuing short-circuits pain, terminates it, or alleviates
it without the rescuee having to do anything to
change. The rescuer takes all the responsibility.

Sometimes that is necessary and good. Sometimes it is not. Let us examine "rescuing" more closely.

The Not-So-Gentle Art of Rescuing*. There are two kinds of "rescuing." There is "rescuing with a small r," and "Rescuing with a big R." The former is what you do for somebody who will be in genuine danger if you don't help him, is in a crisis situation, and is unable to help himself, for example the non-swimmer who is about to drown. That kind of rescuing is humanitarian and deserves a medal.

In contrast, Rescuing (with a capital R) is help that is given when it is not really needed, when the Rescuee would be better off helping himself. The motive of Rescuing is to make the Rescuer feel better about himself, to earn himself a medal or applause or admiration, to make himself "indispensable," and/or keep the Rescued person in a dependent, one-down, helpless position. If the lifesaver later discourages the non-swimmer from learning to swim ("What do you need to do that for? You've got me to save you, and besides, you probably wouldn't be able to learn anyway"), he is no longer a rescuer but has become instead a Rescuer.

The Rescuer is in reality a benevolent despot in the disguise of a humanitarian, deceptively a "gentle" person going around the countryside bestowing blessed relief from pain—and thereby enabling many

---

*For an overview of concepts of Rescuing, see Muriel James and Dorothy Jongeward, *Born to Win*. Reading, MA: Addison-Wesley Publishing Co., 1971.

people to continue longer and longer in a destructive pattern that will end in a greater, albeit postponed, disaster. The Rescuer is Rescuing himself from deepseated feelings (dimly perceived) of inadequacy, avoiding his own pain of not being needed by making others dependent on him for their comfort, rather than encouraging them to be or become adequate and self-reliant. Insecure, the Rescuer requires frequent proof of being OK, by being everybody's friend, pleasing everyone, caring for them in order to be loved back. The Rescuer's motivation is his *own* need rather than the need of the Rescuee.

To Rescue someone is actually a put-down of that person. It is to put one's own needs ahead of the needs of the other person, doing the Rescuing at the expense of the person one is Rescuing. By Rescuing, the Rescuer in fact views the Rescuee as either hopeless, helpless, or inadequate, thereby preserving the needed fantasy that the Rescuer, by contrast, is more powerful and adequate.

Not only is Rescuing a put-down, it is also an unkindness in another way: It prolongs the pain of the Rescuee, by diminishing it to a dull ache which never ends. It is like putting a band-aid and some novacaine on gangrene. It is a form of "Pleasure Principle" behavior: "Above all, let's all be comfortable now—the hell with the future." It is kinder, in the tradition of "tough love," to allow someone to suffer a sharp but short-lived pain, followed by the exhileration of cure and long-lasting health, than to relegate him to an ongoing, chronic, inescapable dull ache, with possible disaster in the end.

The thought that one can prevent another from feeling pain is an irrational one anyway. Because of its important role in preserving life, pain is inextricably bound up with living. To live is inevitably to feel pain. The only way to avoid it altogether is either to zonk oneself out on drugs to produce continual anaesthesia, or to commit suicide. I would not wish for my child, or my students, a life free from pain—but rather the wisdom and strength and resources to cope with it.

As you apply the methods presented here, and as you begin to face people exhibiting unacceptable behavior and ask them to take responsibility for their behavior and its consequences, you will begin to see the Rescuers appear. Sometimes it will seem as if you are surrounded by them. They may be the people who can't stand "unpleasantness," who want everybody to be instantly happy, who need to be needed and to be liked by everybody and to be everybody's "friend," or they may be the omnipotent and all-powerful ones, whose grandiosity has convinced them that they can make the world all right and take away all the pain.

One reason why you will find them appearing suddenly is because your students, wanting to avoid the pain of confrontation and taking responsibility and facing consequences, will send out an urgent SOS for a Rescue. Troubled students are uncanny at recognizing Rescuers and getting them to Rescue them.

You will be able to cope with the Rescuers who are other students by relabeling, reminding the Rescuees that they are being "easily misled" (a problem on the PPC Problem List), and helping them to be assertive in declining to be "sucked in" to another person's problem. However, the Rescuers who will be the biggest problem for you are your own colleagues.

Rescuers abound in all professions and all walks of life, and teachers are no exception. In fact, teachers, because they deal constantly with children who, by nature of being children, are immature in physical strength, emotions, knowledge, and experience, may be more prone than most to Rescuing. In particular, they may be susceptible to developing a view of finality rather than relativity about their students' strength—that because their strengths are limited now they always will be.

Parents in general are susceptible to the same limited view, continuing to see their offspring as incompetent and inexperienced long after the children have grown up, established their own families, and become respected in their professions. (The father who is a hundred and ten still has more "experience" than his son who is eighty!) But troubled children especially attract and stimulate Rescuers, because they are clearly less competent than their normal peers.

The first time you become aware of a Rescuer may be after you have sent a student to the Holding Room. You will think that you have an understanding with the administrator and your colleagues that

while a student is in the Holding Room he is to be
thinking about getting himself under control enough
to discuss a commitment with you. His problem is
with you, and needs to be focused there.

However, when you arrive you may discover that
a "kindly" colleague is talking earnestly with your
student. The Rescuer may be a male or a female,
possibly even your esteemed administrator himself.
Your contract has been temporarily forgotten in his
anxiety to keep control of things and keep students
in class.

The Rescuer is deeply engaged in a "heart-to-
heart" talk, "trying to help" your student by having
him explain how he feels, listening sympathetically
to how upset he is, how unfairly he has been treated
by one and all—especially you—and how he could
be a model student if only other people (you especially) would only stop being so mean, neglectful,
boring, and withholding of understanding—in short,
if only you could see things the student's way and
behave as he wants. Usually the student will be
sweet and reasonable, you will be an ogre, and the
Rescuer will set out to be the peacemaker who will
get the two of you back together again, with a wee
bit of change (compromise) on both your parts.
"After all, you can both be reasonable, right?"

You can see the outcome of such tactics: The student has been able to slide out of facing up to the
behavior which, if continued, will lead him into a
lifetime of misery. Further, a triangle of roles has
been created: The "Persecutor-Victim-Rescuer"
triangle. It looks like this:

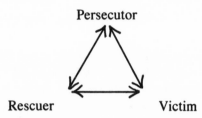

You start out being cast in the role of Persecutor, with the student as the Victim. The Rescuer protects the student from you. However, because the student has not changed and does not follow the Rescuer's "advice" for very long, and therefore gets in trouble again, the Rescuer will keep having to Rescue, and usually eventually feels angry and put-upon, overwhelmed and tired out by having to save so many situations. Then he feels like the Victim ("Everybody always depends on me! Why can't they do something for *me* just once?"), and then in turn becomes the Persecutor ("What's the matter with you people? Can't you do anything right? You just can't manage on your own, can you!"). And so on, round and round, with the roles constantly changing.

If you see this scenario, or variations of it, with interchanging Persecutor-Victim-Rescuer roles, or if you hear angry global statements, including words like "Everybody always. . . ," "Nobody ever. . . ," or if you see a colleague who has special favorites who are under his protection and who stay dependent on him and do not grow and become more adequate, you have a Rescuer in your midst.

Be assertive. Design a DESC script of your own to deal with the situation. Do some problem-solving. Since you cannot change the Rescuer and you can only help the Rescuer change if *he* chooses to, and often Rescuers are having too much fun and gratification from their games to want to stop, you may have to opt for keeping him away from your students until your students are advanced enough to be able to cope with the Rescuer themselves. (You are looking forward to the day when your student says: "Thanks for your offer of help, but I can handle this. My problem is with Mr. ——, and I need to deal with it with him.")

Suggested Exercise: Recognizing Rescuer-Persecutor-Victim Triangles

Introduction to Exercise: *Games* are a ritualized form of human interaction which have a hidden motivation. "Every game is basically dishonest." (Eric Berne, M.D., *Games People Play, The Psychology of Human Relationships,* New York: Grove Press, 1964, p. 48.) A game involves a series of moves with a snare, and a payoff which is often disadvantageous to one of the players, who has been "set up" by another player. Games can be very grim and exhausting. If we do not recognize that we are in a game, our energy can be expended in trying fruitlessly to obtain a legitimate goal while we are being sabotaged by a player who is maneuvering us without our realizing it, in order to obtain his own (secret) goal.

A game can be a way of "using" another person—exploiting him. Being basically dishonest and ritualized, the game prevents intimacy in human relations. Games are of concern in the context of the caring classroom because exploitation, dishonesty, avoidance of intimacy, and wasted energy all work against the establishment of caring relationships.

Since this "game" is a common trap, and one which most people have not been trained to recognize and deal with, we recommend you give it some attention so you can be attuned to identify it easily. If you can identify it when it occurs, you can use your assertiveness skills to deal with it.

1. See if you can identify this game when you observe people interacting with each other. *Check your feelings*. If you are in a "game," your body will usually give you a clue. Common physical responses to "games" are:

   "butterflies" or cramps
   pounding heart
   sweating
   cold feeling
   prickly or tingling feeling
   general discomfort
   rapid breathing

   Common emotional feelings are:

anger
guilt
fear
desire to get away from the situation

Note what is happening when you are aware of these responses.

2. Describe the situation and see if you can identify the roles; often the same person will take different roles. Example:

   a. *Situation*
      The teachers complained to the administrator that a school psychologist was not following agreed-upon policy and procedures in dealing with four students in the past week. They thought what he was doing was harmful to the students. They asked that the administrator talk with the school psychologist because when they approached him individually about the problem he became angry and shouted at them and continued disregarding procedures. The administrator discovered that one of the teachers had referred one student to the psychologist for a problem outside his area of expertise and then was dissatisfied with the action he took. Teachers and psychologist were angry.
   b. *Roles*
      The teachers perceived that they and the students were Victims of the psychologist who

was Persecutor of both the teachers and students. They wanted the administrator to Rescue them and the students. At least one teacher had become a Persecutor of the psychologist who was now the Victim in this transaction. The teachers felt that by their actions they had been Rescuers of the students. Now they wanted the administrator to Persecute the psychologist who would become the Victim. Thus:

Students = Victims (of psychologist)

Teachers =
Victims (of psychologist)
Rescuers (of students)
Persecutor (of psychologist)

Psychologist =
Persecutor (of students and teachers)
Victim (of teachers)
Intended Victim (of administrator, if she plays)

Administrator (depending on what she does) =
Rescuer (of teachers and students)
Persecutor (of psychologist)
Victim (of everybody)
or Assertive problem-solver

3. Identify what assertive solutions are possible to resolve the problem.
4. Choose the solution you prefer (using Classic

Problem-Solving and Assertiveness tools).
5. When you find yourself in a "game," and it is appropriate and comfortable for you to take action, commit your chosen solution to action. (describing what you did and the outcome).
6. Evaluate the outcome. What did you learn about dealing with R-P-V triangles? What might you do differently next time?

Triangling. "Triangling" is a neat trick used by people (all of us do it) when a situation has become so intense that it is uncomfortable.* It is a way of diluting an interaction or relationship between two people. For example, it is often difficult to be intimate. If you and I are in a situation where our conversation is becoming too intimate, and we are getting uncomfortable, one or the other of us may "triangle in" another person. ("Hey, Jane! Come on over and join us. Haven't seen you for awhile. What's new?") People who have just met, avoiding the intimacy of talking about themselves, will "triangle in" the weather, the job, a hobby, how their favorite team is doing, etc. Some family members, not wanting to relate to each other, will triangle in the TV set, the newspaper, or the housework.

The Persecutor-Victim-Rescuer triangle is a variation of the above. It is created in the classroom, for

---

*The concept of triangles is from the theory of intimate relationships, especially family therapy. It has been discussed at length in the work of Murray Bowen, Philip Guerin, et. al., at The Center for Family Learning, New Rochelle, New York.

instance when a problem has arisen in the relationship between you and a student. The student, finding this diad too intense and uncomfortable, looks for a way out by calling for a Rescuer, "triangling" him in. Now you no longer have to deal with each other. Each of you is busy with the new member.

When you are trying to box a student in so he will have to deal with you, watch for his attempts to "triangle." He would rather talk about why the ocean is near the shore than to talk with you about his behavior. He will have to go to the lavatory, or talk about what happened in his early life, or he'll have a stomach ache. Anything to distract you, to get you "off his case."

Understanding how triangles work will help you to recognize them. Assertiveness helps to deal with them because assertiveness allows two people to deal with each other and their feelings and concerns about intimacy in a comfortable, direct way, with much less need to resort to triangling.

In general, you will want to avoid triangles. The problem behavior we are discussing in this book is so difficult and entrenched, that it takes an intense direct relationship to enable change to take place. (The triad is not a triangle, by the way. Rather, it operates in *support* of focus, rather than in diluting of it. Each member relates to each other member in an intense and unique way, rather than using one to avoid relating to another.

If you can avoid triangles and cope with Rescuing, you will have gone far in creating for your students an atmosphere for growth and way of relating directly and honestly that many people do not have the opportunity to enjoy in an entire lifetime.

A Note About Classroom Composition: Sexual Segregation or Integration

Shall you have both boys and girls in your class? This is a question that is often answered too quickly. It bears some thought, as there are arguments pro and con.

If your class is a special education program for students with behavior disorders, and particularly if it is in an institution for the treatment of delinquent youth, make every effort to have your class limited to one sex in the beginning. The reasons for this are explained well and at length by Vorrath and Brendtro in *Positive Peer Culture*.

Briefly, delinquency is largely a product of male cultures, and delinquent males will relate more quickly and fully to their male peers. Inappropriate behavior is often stimulated by adolescent need to impress the girls and vie for them. Conversely, girls develop their sex roles in relation to each other, with peer support and encouragement. They need to be girls with other girls, to develop their identity before risking it with the boys.

Although problems of relating to the opposite sex present opportunities, and need to be dealt with sooner or later, in the beginning they will only dramatically escalate your difficulties when you are still alone in your efforts to establish control, and a fledgeling, caring classroom culture. Once you have control and student helpers, and the caring culture is well established in your classroom, you can begin to introduce students of the opposite sex. I have had good results doing it this way.

If your class is a "regular" class in a regular community school setting, and you have troubled children in it along with "normal" children, you need not be concerned about the mixing of sexes—your class will be mixed already and there is no need to change it. The normally-behaving students will quickly provide the needed support.

Daniel Fader, in *Hooked on Books,* presents in some detail his reasons for believing that the sexes ought to be integrated: The ("pushy") boys take the active roles in class, and the less assertive girls are lost, pushed back to a passive role where they receive less recognition and attention. Yet, the girls are usually the better students and much more facile with words. In a mixed class, in mixed triads, the girls receive stimulus and recognition for more adequate, active participation, and the boys benefit from the girls' sharing of their word skills. These benefits are more relevant to academic considerations, but obviously have affective ramifications as well.

Although a minority of delinquent students can totally disrupt a regular class, the delinquent culture is not usually entrenched. Therefore, once you have established control and your methods are taking hold, the affective education of the students is enhanced by their being able to relate to each other in direct, assertive, caring, appropriate ways, with your supervision and guidance. Because of the mutual benefits to both boys and girls, Fader counts as one of his highest priorities the inclusion of one member of the opposite sex in each triad.

Thus, your decision to integrate or not will depend on several factors: the location of your class, whether it is "special" or "regular" in character, the percentage of delinquent members, and how securely you have established your system and a firm caring culture. An additional factor, of course, is the agreement of your administrator with your decision, and the presence of resources to enable the existence of a segregated or integrated class.

Affective Education and Drug Abuse (a Special Issue)

Drug and alcohol (mostly alcohol) abuse is epidemic in this country, and a large proportion of the behavior schools find intolerable is due to this plague. Many of the students are themselves addicted, and many of those who are not yet addicted are showing the devastating effects of having addicted parents.

As teachers, you will not be giving specific drug and alcohol* abuse "treatment." For that there are

---

*Many people, teachers included, do not realize that alcohol is a drug. Not only is it a drug, but it is one of the most potent, addicting, and dangerous of all drugs and is the primary drug abused by young people.

people trained specifically in that field. Many states have special certification of alcoholism counselors, recognized by third-party payers such as Blue Cross. Alcoholics Anonymous, Al-Anon, and Ala-teen are the national self-help groups, for people of all ages who abuse or are addicted to alcohol, and for their families and friends. Become familiar with the programs and helping professionals and groups in your area, for consultation and referral. Your school may have a program for students who abuse drugs.

You *will* be working toward drug and alcohol abuse *prevention,* however, because all of the methods presented in this book give students healthy ways of dealing with problems; and having such resources, they may be less likely to abuse drugs as a way of resolving their problems. There are many reasons why youngsters abuse drugs. These methods specifically address some of them.

However, if a youngster is already addicted to alcohol or other drugs, you cannot rely on the methods presented here to overcome the addiction. People used to believe that alcoholism, for example, was a symptom of an underlying personality disorder: If the underlying disorder were treated, and cured, the alcoholism would go away—because the person would no longer need to drink. Now it is known that that view is false—alcoholism is not a symptom but a primary illness with many causes, some of which are biochemical, possibly biogenetic, and possibly allergic. The crazy behavior you see may well be a symptom of the primary underlying

illness of alcoholism which, if undetected or un-
treated, will eventually kill its victim. Alcoholism is
a progressive and fatal illness which maims and de-
stroys many young lives.

Alcoholism is also an *addiction*. In an addictive
process, the body makes changes to adjust to the
frequent or prolonged introduction into it of an addictive substance. For example, alcohol is a depressant. It depresses the body functions. Just as when
it is cold outside we turn up the heat and when it is
hot outside we turn on the air-conditioner, in order
to maintain a steady level of comfort when the body
is consistently receiving a depressant, it begins to
speed up in order to overcome the effects of the
drug. Thus, when the effects of the drug wear off,
the changes the body has made can be seen—"with-
drawal symptoms," such as the shakes or DT's or,
in mildest form, restlessness, sweats, and inability
to sleep. Now the sufferer has to take another drink
(or another depressant drug) to stop the symptoms,
or, to put it another way, he must drink to get well.

Once a person is addicted, no amount of "improved self image" or other responsible behavior,
will interrupt the addiction. In fact, improved self-
respect and responsible behavior is impossible to
achieve while the person remains addicted. Only
after the person *stops* taking the addicting substance
can recovery begin. The first goal is to stop the addiction. The person must stop taking the drug, and
remain abstinent from it, in order to get better.
Then, and only then, can the methods presented

here help the person to remain abstinent and to re-cover.

Never underestimate the power of the addiction. Never ignore or minimize or overlook it if you know or suspect* that one of your students is drinking or taking non-prescribed or illegal drugs. Do not accept or fall for his denial or promises to "quit tomorrow." Always get him referred for treatment or to an AA group, or both. Do not rely on your own teaching methods to interrupt his drug abuse. If the behavior that is of concern to the school is related in any way to the abuse of drugs (including alcohol), it will not change through any of the methods discussed here, until the drug use is first stopped.

"Is that the responsibility of the teacher—to get a student referred for drug treatment?" you may ask. If not the teacher, then who? Who knows the student better, is more objective, has the best opportunity to observe him? His parents may be addicted themselves, or deeply into a denial process, or absent altogether. If not now, when? After he is so deeply into his addiction that permanent irreversible damage has occurred? After he's dead?

Some of your troubled students will not yet be addicted, but will be abusing drugs occasionally or even regularly—"playing around" with them. And some will be suffering the results of having lived

---

*Become familiar with the symptoms of drug and alcohol abuse. If you see the symptoms, do not ignore them. Assertively address the issue with the student. Consult with professionals and refer the student to professionals who can deal with his denial.

with addicted parents. Your understanding of the problem, your knowledge of it, will be of enormous help to them, both because of your being free to talk about it without any need to put them or their parents down, or to discount how deeply they hurt, and because of the correct information you can give them and the misinformation you can correct.

Despite extensive experience with drugs, youth are abominably ignorant about them (alcohol especially), and about their short and long-term effects. (Drugs affect young people very differently from the way they effect adults, yet youngsters expect to drink the same way they see adults drink, with devastating, often fatal, results.)

Don't let them down. Get all the information you can, and supplement it with the use of consultants, friends in the drug/alcohol field, including recovered people, who will be willing to join you in some of your discussions with your class.

Literature is available from Alcoholics Anonymous, the National Institute on Alcohol Abuse and Alcoholism (NIAAA), The National Institute of Drug Abuse (NIDA), The National Council on Alcoholism, and your state health department or Regional Council on Alcoholism. Get it and share it with your students. Some addresses for information are:

Alcoholics Anonymous
P.O. Box 459
Grand Central Station
New York, N.Y. 10163

Al-Anon
P.O. Box 182
Madison Square Station
New York, N.Y. 10159

National Council on Alcoholism (NCA)—a voluntary, non-governmental agency
733 Third Avenue
New York, N.Y. 10017
(Directory of local affiliates may be obtained by writing NCA)

National Clearinghouse for Alcohol Information (NCALI)—a service of the National Institute on Alcohol Abuse & Alcoholism (NIAAA) of the U.S. Dept. of Health & Human Services—a source of free information on alcohol related subjects, posters, pamphlets, referral sources, etc.
P.O. Box 2345
Rockville, Md. 20852

National Institute on Drug Abuse (NIDA)
5600 Fishers Lane
Rockville, Md. 20857

Racial Integration of Schools and the Caring Classroom

It is common to hear of newly integrated school systems in which *de facto* segregation continues, with white students congregating with each other and black students with each other in obvious separate groups, and with administrators, faculty, and students not knowing quite what to do about it. The caring classroom model lends itself naturally to the integrating process, both in preparation for the advent of racial integration and in accomplishing a truly integrated educational system in actual practice. Because caring is the norm, students can be prepared in advance for the coming of new members of class, and for dealing appropriately with feelings about newness and change.

Problems are opportunities in the case of racial integration just as in any other situation. In forming the triads, the teacher factors in race as an additional piece of data, integrating the triads wherever possible.

"Mainstreaming" Students with Handicaps

The same principles hold true for mainstreaming of students with handicaps. Children are acutely aware of differences; sometimes they react to others' handicaps with fear and alarm, sometimes avoiding or teasing the person with a handicap.

Parents of handicapped children may be concerned about how their children will be received when mainstreamed. The practices of preparing the class in advance, and then introducing the handicapped student into a triad, help the students become comfortable with each other. These practices also help the handicapped students to become quickly integrated into the classroom, while giving them intense support from the other members of the triad. Furthermore, the handicapped student has the opportunity quickly to be a helping, contributing member of the class through his own role in the triad.

As the students get to know each other, and appreciate each other's strengths through the work in the triad, the differences become no longer strange and frightening. Mutual respect, seeing each other as people, and treating each other with caring and kindness are the result.

Suggested Readings

Berne, Eric, M.D. *Games People Play.* New York: Grove Press, 1964.
On Transactional Analysis. See pp. 85–91 for "Now I've Got You, You Son of a Bitch."

Harris, Thomas A., M.D. *I'm OK—You're OK.* New York: Harper and Row, 1969.
Transactional Analysis.

James, Muriel, and Jongeward, Dorothy. *Born to Win.* Reading, Mass.: Addison-Wesley, 1971.
This is a book which not only gives an overview of concepts (such as P-A-C ego states, OKness, games, and the Victim/Persecutor/Rescuer roles), but also some exercizes and experiments to do.

Alberti, R. E., and Emmons, M. L. *Your Perfect Right: A Guide to Assertive Behavior.* San Luis Obispo, Calif.: Impact, 1974.

Bower, S. A., and Bower, G. H. *Asserting Yourself, A Practical Guide for Positive Change.* Reading, Mass.: Addison-Wesley, 1976.
Contains assertiveness problems and practice exercizes.

Cheek, Donald K. *Assertive Black . . . Puzzled White.* San Luis Obispo, Calif.: Impact, 1976.
This book, from the black perspective, gives examples of assertiveness situations applicable to

the black experience. It gives training instruction, steps, questionnaires, and inventories. It should be studied by anyone teaching self-assertion to blacks.

Jakubowski, P., and Lange, A. J. *The Assertive Option, Your Rights and Responsibilities*. Champaign, Ill.: Research Press, 1978.
Philosophy of assertiveness and exercizes and models.

Lange, A. J., and Jakubowski, P. *Responsible Assertive Behavior, Cognitive/Behavioral Procedures for Trainers*. Champaign, Ill.: Research Press, 1976.

Smith, Manuel. *When I Say No I Feel Guilty*. New York: Dial Press, 1975.
This is a popular book on assertiveness for the general public. The reader will note that in the Caring Classroom we take a different view of the assertive right to say "I don't care."

Goldstein, Arnold P., Sprafkin, Robert P., Gershaw, N. Jane, and Klein, Paul. *Skillstreaming the Adolescent, A Structured Learning Approach to Teaching Prosocial Skills*. Champaign, Ill.: Research Press, 1980.
A book of exercizes, useful in teaching assertiveness.

Morse, William C., et. al. *Affective Education for Special Children and Youth*. Reston, Va: The Council for Exceptional Children, 1980.

Pearson, Craig. *Resolving Classroom Conflict*. Palo Alto, Calif.: Learning Handbooks, 1974.
A book of strategies.

Vorrath, Harry and Brendtro, Larry K. *Positive Peer Culture*, 2nd ed. Aldine, Hawthorne, NY: 1984.
See also: Brendtro, Larry K., and Ness, Arlin E. *Re-Educating Troubled Youth, Environments for Teaching and Treatment*. Hawthorne, N.Y.: Aldine, 1983.

Wheelis, Allen. *How People Change*. New York: Harper and Row, 1970.

Yalom, Irvin D., M.D. *The Theory and Practice of Group Psychotherapy*. New York: Basic Books, 1975.

6. The Teacher as a Member of a Multidisciplinary Team

*I*f you are a teacher in a treatment institution, you will be a member of a multidisciplinary team consisting of all the people responsible for the care and treatment of your students: the medical and psychiatric staff, the cottage or group life staff, the psychologists, social workers, recreational and occupational therapists, dietician, etc. If you are a teacher in a regular school, concerned about one or more troubling students, chances are you will still be a member of a multi-disciplinary team that will include at least one other discipline, such as the guidance counselor or school psychologist, perhaps a school social worker, medical or psychiatric consultants, substance abuse counselors, even probation officers and other juvenile court staff. Each member of the team is responsible for bringing his special knowledge and skills to bear on the individual student in a manner that produces a planned, integrated

179

multifaceted approach that would be impossible for one professional alone.

There should be in effect a plan to help each troubled student. There are several steps in developing and carrying out such a helping plan, and the membership of the team may change with each step. For example, the teacher and psychologist may work together at the assessment stage, but the teacher alone may carry out the remedial plan that results.

I have spent years as a member of treatment teams, both as a member of institution group life staff, as an administrator in charge of the treatment program, and as a teacher. My experience has taught me the importance of a system in which people work together to decide what the problem is, what to do about it, and how to know if it worked.

Years ago, people thought that "good intentions" were sufficient—that if a child were surrounded by good people, the benefits would flow to him and be self-evident. However, the ballooning expense of both education and treatment, along with the obvious and frightening problems and failures of education, has made a pained public suspicious. Their skepticism has resulted in a sensitivity to the need to be accountable: What *are* we doing for children? What works? What doesn't? How can we prove it?

For the teacher, there is an even more immediate basic question: What am *I* going to do that will help this student? How does what I do fit with what others are doing? Are we working at cross-purposes?

It is a professional responsibility to know what we have to offer, how to collaborate with others, and how to know whether or not we have been successful.

Team Collaboration on a Plan

The Data Base. The first step in team collaboration is to gather data. Data consists of facts and information.* There are two general categories of data: (1) There is *subjective data:* what the child says about himself, his feelings, and his experiences, and the feelings he arouses in others. (2) There is *objective data:* the child's appearance and behavior; medical data about his physical condition; psychiatric or psychological data about his mental functioning and his attitude and mood; social data about his family and peer relationships, milieu, and economic situation; educational data about his school status, achievements, learning patterns, strengths and disabilities.

Assessing the Data. Data is of no worth unless it has meaning. The members of the team decide what the meaning of the data is. This process is called the "assessment"—it is the "so what" aspect of the data. The assessors place a value on the data, deciding if

---

*"Data" is a plural noun; however, we use the word colloquially here, as it is commonly used "in the field" by practitioners, in the singular—indicating *a collection* (sing.) of data.

any aspect of it represents a strength to be supported or a problem to be remedied. (Sometimes data has no meaning at all. For example, the fact that the student was placed in a yellow squad car when he was arrested has no meaning, unless it is a clue in a mystery novel. Experienced professionals will know what data is irrelevant. Inexperienced people will not always know how to decide). A good question to ask in assessing data is, "So what?" How can this information be *used* to help the child? What can we *do* with it? What impact will it have on our plan and his improvement; will it help or hinder recovery or progress? If it can't be used, it may be nothing more than gossip.

Developing a Plan. The plan is the answer to the double question: "What are we going to do about what we have decided are the problems, and how are we going to support the strengths?" There are several parts to the plan, including:

a. *The goals*—what we want to achieve;
b. *The interventions*—specifically what we will do to achieve each goal;
c. *The measures of success*—how we will know (in measurable terms) when we have accomplished the goal or successfully completed the intervention;
d. *The time frame*—by what date or within what period of time we will have done it;
e. *The assignment of responsibility*—who (which member of the team) will do it;

f. *The update*—by what date this *plan will be up- dated* or *finally evaluated.*

All members of the team must be aware of the plan and of their respective responsibilities.* To en- sure this, and to ensure that all members understand the plan, agree with it, and are able to carry out their responsibilities, all members should participate in the formulation of the plan.

Troublesome snags can appear if somebody is as- signed a responsibility by others who do not consult him. He may not agree, or the skill may be outside his expertise or present him with an ethical or prac- tical problem he cannot surmount, or he simply may not be aware of the responsibility—it is too easy to assume that someone else is taking care of the com- munication. Courtesy, efficiency, and practicality all dictate that those who are to carry out the plan be involved in the design of it, or at least be consulted for their agreement.

Updating the Plan. For any plan that consists of more than a brief discrete intervention, and that will be implemented over a period of at least several

---

*Since the plan is for the student's benefit, and he will be operating within it, it stands to reason that he should be con- sulted as it is being designed. At the very least, if his coopera- tion is not forthcoming, it should be explained to him. The student is as much a member of the team as anyone else. He should be included, also, in any discussion updating the plan, and in evaluating his progress.

weeks, there should be a provision for updating. Updating consists of:

a. consideration of what has been accomplished to this point,
b. assessment of any new data (what has been learned since the initial plan was made), and any changes it may require in the original assessment and goals,
c. what still remains to be accomplished in relation to the original goals,
d. any new goals (with their attendant interventions, measures of success, and assignments of responsibility), and
e. the next date when the plan will be updated.

Final Summary or Transfer Summary. If responsibility for the student is being transferred to another team, or if the plan is accomplished, the team, consisting of those members remaining active or responsible, should do a final summary of the implementation of the plan. This summary includes progress toward attaining each goal, any final conclusions, and any recommendations about uncompleted goals or unresolved problems.

If you are a member of a new team receiving such a summary, that summary will be part of the data base for your new assessment and plan. You and your team will be responsible for considering it and making any changes that in your professional judgment are indicated. And so the process goes on.

The Written Record

In the arena of accountability, it is often declared, "If it isn't written down, it hasn't happened." You and your team need a system of record-keeping that will enable you to keep track of what you are doing, help you to evaluate it, and that will communicate the assessment, plan, and point of progress to anyone taking your place, particularly in case of a sudden interruption of responsibility. You don't want all your good work for the child to be lost if something happens to you or he is suddenly transferred to a different locale.

The Progress Note. After experimenting with and seeing many types of record-keeping over the years, I find that I prefer an adaptation from the "Problem Oriented Medical Record"* for keeping current progress notes—the so-called "SOAP" format of notemaking. Not everybody likes this format, and you may not like it either. If you have a better way, by all means use it. I like the SOAP format because it helps to focus, to keep out extraneous irrelevant material, and to keep records brief and easily readable.

SOAP is an acronym for the followng: S = Subjective (what the student says); 0 = Objective (what I have observed, the facts); A = Assessment (what I think is the significance) of the data in S and O; P = the plan (what I am going to do about it).

---

*A format used in many hospitals for keeping medical charts.

Example: I may have a note in my folder on a student that looks like this:

2/25/8   10 AM
S— "Leave me alone. I don't feel well."
O— Falling asleep in class. Irritable when spoken to. Hands trembling. Sweating. Smell of alcohol on breath.
A— Alcohol problem
P— Request psychological and medical consultation for assessment of problem and plan for referral if indicated. Sent to school nurse for immediate aid.

The Multidisciplinary Assessment and Plan. While I find the SOAP note useful for brief progress notes, more is needed for the multidisciplinary assessment and plan. Figure 6 is an example (from a fictitious case of a student in an institution—the process would be the same, if the student were in a community school, although of course the details would be different).

The beauty of this format is that it is brief, concise, flows logically from one part to the next, and almost automates the thinking process. It is the simplest and most painless format I have found.

Few professionals actually like record-keeping; it tends to be seen as a necessary evil. It behooves us to make it as useful and painless as possible. If we give it the thought and time it deserves, it will reward us—making us more clear-thinking and responsible in what we do with and for our students.

A Word About the IEP

There are books written about how to do an Individualized Educational Plan (IEP), and there is no reason to go into detail here. Each district or state will have guidelines for complying with the law, and consultation available on how to apply the guidelines.

The IEP requires a multidisciplinary assessment and recommendations. The teacher who first recognizes an unusual behavior problem in a student initiates the process, and thereby finds himself on a multidisciplinary team.

Although guidelines for IEP's differ, the process presented here will be generally applicable to the development of any IEP.

Introduction to Forms. The following four forms are examples of how to document the work of the team.

1. The first form (figure 4) is a way of presenting the preliminary data, gathered by a multidisciplinary team, in summary form. It consists of what is known initially about the student (the "data base"), with little if any evaluation of the significance of the data.
2. The second form (figure 5) is the documentation of the team's beginning evaluation ("assessment") of the data: the significance that they attach, in their professional judgment, to the data, their conclusions about it, and their thoughts on the effect (negative or positive) the data may have on the student's progress and treatment. This serves as the impetus for the plan. It is the "so-what?" aspect of the data.

   This represents a difficult step because it takes thought and commits one to a conclusion. There is always a temptation

187

merely to repeat the data rather than taking a chance on stating its significance. Also, people tend to avoid assessments early in the process, fearing making a mistake. Do not be concerned: The update can take into account new data and correct any misdiagnoses. You are not expected to know everything or see into the future.

3. The third form (figure 6) is in fact a continuation on the back of the figure 5 form. It is the plan, based on the assessment of the data. The goals are indicated first, identified according to the numbers of the problems or strengths on the assessment form.

   In this example, the first goals are identified as "2" which relates to "physical" on the assessment form. Here there are three goals in the "physical" category, a, b, and c. Each goal is followed by the intervention: How will the team reach the goal? What specific action will it take?

   Following each intervention is the measure of the effectiveness of the action. How will the team know if the treatment has worked? These should be written in as concrete

(Introduction to Forms continues on p. 196, following Figures 4 through 7.)

Figure 4. Data Base.

John Petrotunis   *8/23*
SS# *000-00-0000*
DOB: *1970*

Examination by M. D.:
14 year old white male, pale, thin, undernourished, BP normal. Temperature 98.6. Weight: 100 lbs. Systems review negative. Puncture marks on arms. Teeth: many cavities; inflamed gums. Signs of shaking/tremors on admission. Admits to past occasional use of heroin, amphetamines; alcohol daily. Fingernails are bitten to quick. Impression: Malnutrition, drug and alcohol abuse, dental disease, anxiety neurosis.

Nursing Notes:
Quiet, polite on admission. Gross tremors of hands. Admits to using alcohol (wine, beer, occasional whiskey). Seems withdrawn.

Social Worker:
Parents divorced. Father's whereabouts unknown. Mother alcoholic. John has lived in a series of foster homes where he usually is ingratiating for awhile and then displays problems, such as bullying the younger children, truancy, defiance of authority, stealing. Recently he was away from F. H. for 2 days and was caught by police attempting to burglarize an occupied building at night. F. H. has refused to have him back. Mother is currently hospitalized with chronic liver disease.

School History:
John completed 3rd grade in Steeltown prior to his parent's divorce. His grades were average or slightly below. He had a short attention span and was a slow reader. School performance and attendance has been patchy since, due to frequent moves and truancy. Grade level overall is 6.1. He has shown interest and skill in drawing and music, generally poor performance in reading, spelling, composition and math. John wore glasses at one time but stopped wearing them about 4 years ago. He has few friends, being rather a loner and unaccepted by other students. He formed a close relationship with his music teacher last year and she thinks he has some talent.

Psychological:
John was withdrawn and wary during the interview and testing situation. He is socially and emotionally immature, with few coping skills. He seems to be fearful about what is going to happen to him, but does not show his feelings. He appears somewhat depressed. He is small for his age. IQ (full scale)—90 (possibly would do better under more comfortable circumstances).

Transition Cottage Staff Notes:
John wet the bed the first 2 nights, and once the end of the week. He is polite and helpful to staff, avoids the other boys.

Figure 5. Initial Team Assessment.

Prepared by: *S. Soho, Social Worker, for the team*   9/1

Circle problem areas and list them on back in "Goals" column:

Assessment From Data (Include strengths as well as problems)

1. Reason for referral to Program: *Stealing, burglary, out of control, homeless, truant, drug-abuser, generally irresponsible non-conforming lifestyle; unresponsive to discipline and authority.*

Problem

2. Physical: *Underweight, needs dental care (gums and cavities). Insufficient data: cause of tremors? Needs more physical workup. Rule out detoxifying from recent drugs? Alcoholic? Rule out need for glasses.*

Problem

3. Attitude/Psychological: *Anxious, tense, wary, problems coping (drug abuse, truancy) with interpersonal relationships. Insight? (unknown) Cooperative. Rule out depression (may be reactive). Low self-esteem, interferes with coping and relating. Judgement poor.*

Problem

4. Family: *Non-supportive, not a resource. Foster home probably not a resource either. No supportive network in the community (except possibly music teacher). Generally isolated from caring adults. Serious problem which will retard progress unless addressed.*

Problem—Strength

5. Education: *Behind in school about 3 years — probably due to social and emotional problems. Normal I. Q. Needs educational diagnostic profile. Strength: has musical talent. Assess artistic interest and ability which might give him some satisfaction, self-esteem and recognition.*

Problem

⑥ Socio-cultural/Environmental: *No permanent residence (foster homes in past). Loner. No strong ethnic ties for support. No religious or spiritual background as source of strength. Needs to develop a lifestyle and environmental supports for progress.*

Problem

⑦ Relationships: *No peer relationships. Cautious with adults. Withdrawn—which contributes to apparent depression.*

Strength

⑧ Interests/Skills: *Musical talent. Possible artistic skill and interest may be a means of reaching him, increasing self-esteem and contact with peers and adults.*

Problem

⑨ Other: *Needs alcoholism and drug education, and A A, as he appears to have no understanding of abuse, addiction/recovery.*

Diagnostic Impression:

1. *Physical—Underweight, drug (incl. alc.) abuser (possibly addicted), dental disease.*

2. *Psycho-Social—Immature, lacks interpersonal coping skills, probably depressed; homeless.*

3. *Educational—Educationally retarded & normal intelligence.*

Student Name and Identifying Data: *John Petrolunis*
SS# 000-00-000 DOB: 1970

Joseph Paine, M.D.—physician
S. Nightingale, R. N.—Nurse
R. Smith—Cottage 3—Child Care Worker
S. Philo—teacher
S. Loho, MSW—Social Worker
B. White, CAC—alc. Counselor

Figure 6. Treatment Plan.

	Goals (Keyed to Number on front of Form)	Intervention
②	a) Weight gain to normal (ideal) for age/height	Special diet
	b) Observe for detoxification from recent (current?) drug use	Urine screening, staff observation and referral to M.D. if symptoms increase
	c) Oral health (fillings, treatment of gums?)	Referral to dentist
③⑦	Adequate interpersonal skills	Positive peer culture, assertiveness training
④⑥	Develop community supports to replace absent family	Evaluate option of group home placement
⑤	Long-Term: Improve reading, writing, spelling math, social studies to grade level 9.0	Assignment to triad, programmed learning plan
	Short-term: Complete Educational Diagnostic Profile	Ed. Dx. Profile
⑧	Support musical talent	Volunteer/music lessons
⑨	Abstinence from alcohol and non-prescribed drugs	Alcohol and Drug abuse ed. AA meetings

Signed (Must be signed by all staff having responsibility):

Joseph Paine, M.D., S. Nightingale, R.N., R. Smith, Child
Care Worker, S. Philo, Teacher, S. Soho, MSW, B. White, CAC
This plan will be updated on: 9/15 11/15 _____ _____

192

Measures of Treatment Effectiveness	Time Frame or Date of Expected Outcome	Staff Responsibility
Achieves ideal weight	5 lbs. within 2 months; referral to dietitian this week	Dietitian, Dr. P., Mrs. Nightingale
Symptoms subside and eventually no sign of drug use. If symptoms continue, complete referral	Within 2 weeks	Mr. Smith Mr. Smith
Completion of dental treatment	Referred to Dr. O this week	Mr. Smith, Dr. O.
Observed improved peer intervention; no school absence due to coping problems; symptoms of depression subside	9 months	Mr. Smith Mr. Philo
Decision, acceptable to John, of appropriate placement	Within 9 months	Mrs. Soho
Achieves grade level	To be determined at next update	Mr. Philo
Profile and individualized ed. goals and plan	One week	Mr. Philo
Subjective satisfaction	2 months	Mrs. Soho
No symptoms of alcohol or other abuse	During stay at this institution and aftercare	Mrs. White, CAC

This plan was discussed with student on __9/2__.

Staff signature __R. Smith, Child Care Worker__

Student Signature __John Petrotunis__

193

Figure 7. Ongoing Team Assessment and Treatment Plan

Prepared by: *R. Smith, Recorder for the team*   9/15

<u>Data</u> since last assessment & plan: (continue on back)

② a) *Weight gain of 3 lbs. Instructed in diet; understands diet.*

     b) *Restlessness at night. Bedwetting ceased. No tremulousness since 9/4. Urine + for marijuana.*

     c) *Referral to dentist completed. Examination complete. Treatment instituted 9/9.*

③⑦ *Essentially unchanged.*

④⑥ *No new data.*

  ⑤ *E.D.P completed. Goals and plan attached.*

  ⑧ *Volunteer has been contacted.*

  ⑨ *Referral to drug education program made. A.A volunteer contacted.*

<u>Assessment</u> of new data: (continue on back)

② a) *Plan progressing well with diet — cooperative*

     b) *Uneventful detoxification. Marijuana abuse in past (inconclusive how recent) — no evidence of present use.*

     c) *Plan progressing well.*

③⑦ *Wary and isolated.*

④⑥ *None. Plan not yet instituted.*

  ⑤ *Plan progressing on schedule. Student taking "wait and see" attitude, fearful of revealing himself yet, cautious, compliant.*

  ⑧ *Plan progressing.*

  ⑨ *Plan progressing.*

194

Update of Plan (include new goals from above data/assessment)—Continue on back

Goals (by corresponding no.)	Intervention	Measures of Prescribed Effectiveness	Time Frame	Staff Responsibility
② a) unchanged ⟶				

no new goals at
this time

Staff Signatures: *Joseph Paine, M.D., F. Nightingale, R.N.*
R. Smith, Child Care Worker, G. Philo, Teacher, S. Soho,
MSW, B. White, CAC

See Initial Treatment Plan for time of next update.

behavioral terms as possible. The next column specifies the time by which the action will be taken or completed. The last column identifies specifically what staff member (by name) will be responsible for each action.

Note that the form is signed by each person having responsibility, indicating his knowledge of his responsibility and concurrence with it. Equally important is the student's signature that he is familiar with the plan.

4. The last form (figure 7) documents further data gathered as the team comes to know the student and his circumstances better, assessment of this new data, and update of the plan based on this additional or changed assessment. The timing of this update may be dictated by agency policy. Updating should be done at regular intervals and as needed.

For example, sometimes (not in this illustration) new data will completely change a plan and make it necessary to suspend the former goals temporarily or permanently. Such instances would be sudden serious illness, appearance of dangerous explosiveness in a previously passive-compliant student, the appearance of a previously unknown but significant relative, an unexpected change in the family which has a significant impact on the case, etc. In cases like these, the plan should be immediately updated, without waiting until a predetermined date.

Note: The examples used here are from institutional settings, but these forms can be used in any setting.

7. Aftercare: There Is Life after Your Classroom

*D*oes the caring just happen <u>inside</u> the classroom—just <u>stay</u> there? Or does it begin to generalize? Do your students ever start to care in other places too?

I was asked these questions by a new principal, after about two months into a new school year. My class was orderly, the students relaxed. A substitute teacher had spent a day observing in my classroom and was charmed by the way the students helped each other, noticing, for instance, how important it had been to the members of one triad that one of their group grasp the mysteries of the common denominator.

My class was an island of quiet, noticeable because I don't keep the door closed—while most of the school suffered in almost constant turmoil. But when my students left my class to go to another activity, some of them raised all kinds of Cain—just as if they'd never heard of caring. The questions were fair ones.

It is sobering to think how much these students have to overcome, how much they have to learn, in a very short time. They come to you usually with years of bad behavioral habits, and deplorable outlook—getting worse each year.

You may have them eight months. To be sure, you may have them for an intensive eight months, but that is still a very small percentage of their lives in which to overcome the accumulations of a lifetime of poor learning and mislearning.

The answer to the questions is, nevertheless, yes. In most cases the caring does generalize—not for the first few months, usually, but eventually. Patience and preparation for the future are essential to ensure that it does happen.

The caring spreads in concentric rings. First, a student will care about me and gradually about each member of his triad. He may have to concentrate hard—practicing caring against considerable opposition—to care about a member of his triad.

Case illustration: Joe asked to talk with me. He couldn't stand Jack, a member of his triad.

"I can't help it. He bugs the shit out of me! He's so dumb! And he's a jerk! A real turkey!"

"I know it's hard for you to like Jack. I know some of the things he does can drive you up the wall. But are you saying that because he has problems he doesn't deserve to be helped?"

"No. I guess I'm not. . . . But sometimes I can't stand him!"

198

"I know. What do you think you could do when you feel that way?"

"I don't know. I really don't!"

"Shall we see if we can figure out a few things you could do, so you won't feel so mad and can continue to help him?"

"Yeah . . . OK."

In the next progression a student will start to be helpful, considerate, caring toward other members of the class. Then, sooner or later, most will report how they were caring toward a member of their family with whom they had previously been having a conflict. And eventually, most will display responsible behavior toward other faculty and other school students and personnel.

When I know that a student will be leaving my class for good before long, I intensify my "combat training" regimen to prepare him for independent life on his own in "the real world." First, I make certain that he has some assignments outside my class, especially with teachers that are unsympathetic and uncaring—the worse the better! When the student complains, I remind him that he is going to meet many people like that in his lifetime and he'd better learn how not to let them push his buttons and get him to behave in self-defeating ways. At the same time I work intensively with the student, discussing with him the problems he is having with the other teacher, and how he can deal constructively with them.

Within the class itself, I begin to put more responsibility on the student. When he asks me for help or for conference time, I withhold myself. Whereas I usually have in the past negotiated a time for him, I will now turn him down flat, saying I don't have the time. At first, typically, the student won't accept this.

"Whattaya mean, Mr. Carducci?"
"I mean it, George. I'm busy."
"Aw, come on. That's not like you! How about later?"
"No. I'm sorry. You're going to have to deal with it. I don't have the time."
"Shit! What's goin on?"

I will then explain to the student that he is soon going to be up against this kind of problem. How will he deal with it? Will he treat the teacher with disrespect, forgetting the assertiveness rights, or will he handle it in a responsible, self-respecting and other-respecting way? I remind him that he has resources—his peers, his assertiveness tools, his problem-solving skills. I challenge him to use them. Most will quickly and proudly rise to the challenge.

Case illustration: The phone rang at my home after supper one evening. It was Tony, one of my former students who had been "mainstreamed" back into his community school some time before. He was so excited and proud of himself that he'd had to call and tell me what had happened.

His new math teacher was "a bastard"—wouldn't give Tony the time of day—knew Tony "from before." (Tony is a delinquent who had earned considerable notoriety in the school.) Tony was having trouble with the math, couldn't understand it, was falling behind. When he raised his hand, the teacher overlooked him. Tony began to get discouraged, then scared, then angry. He could feel his old sullenness and "don't care" defiance creeping back. But he didn't want that anymore.

He thought the problem over, casting about for a solution, and found one. He remembered the triads, students helping students.

"Today, I raised my hand and stood up in class. I said, 'Excuse me, Mr. Smith, but I've got something to say that's important to me.' I looked around the room at the other students and I said, 'I'm having a lot of trouble understanding this math, and I wonder if any one of you would be willing to work with me to help me with it?'

"And you know what, Mr. Carducci? A whole bunch of kids said they'd be willing to help me! And I met with two of them after class already! I'm not going to get licked by this math or by Mr. Smith!"

"Congratulations, Tony! What did Mr. Smith do?"

"Oh, he said, 'OK—that's a good idea.' He seemed surprised."

"I bet he was! That was just great!"

Imagine the courage it took for Tony—not to be discouraged by his past reputation or by the teacher's not helping or caring—not to revert back to the old familiar behavior patterns "because the world is unfair and nobody cares," to admit before his peers that he didn't understand the math and to ask them to help him, to take care of himself when nobody else was helping, to maintain his self-respect when it would have been so easy to lose it. What a shining success!

The importance of it—the victory of what he had done—was not lost on Tony, and he wanted to share it with me because he knew that I, too, would understand its full meaning. Tony is truly in control of himself now, able to solve his own problems in a healthy way. Independent of me! This victory will remain with him, giving him added courage for the next one, and the next.

What if Tony later becomes inundated? What of those students who are not as ready as Tony to manage on an ongoing basis, day after day, in a "regular" class or with teachers who operate contrary to the concepts and tools recommended in this book? I strongly recommend a lifeline, a contingency plan, or, best yet, an "Aftercare Classroom."

As you can see from the conversation with Tony, I give my home phone number to those students who I think need it, want it, and will use it. Many teachers will not want to do that, and it of course must be an individual choice. If a student really wants to get in touch with you, he will find a way. Some students, to whom I have not given my home phone number, have (very appropriately) called me at school. One memorable student located me on my honeymoon in a hotel even my family didn't know about. Such resourcefulness must be admired even if not welcomed.

When my former students are "mainstreamed" within the same school, I have an arrangement with the administration and faculty that if they begin to show signs of wear and tear, and symptoms of possible relapse are appearing, they can return to my classroom, as a "time-out" area or for some crisis-intervention problem-solving.

Sometimes this is formally planned. Sometimes it is very informal: My former student will appear at the door, nod to me, and take a seat quietly in the "time-out" area while I go on with my teaching. He may sit there thinking, observing the triads at work for awhile, and then quietly leave again. Or he may wait until class is over and then ask me for some conference time.

One of the most tragic things is to see students from institutions immediately mainstreamed. It is cruel. For the student who has been in an institution and who abruptly returns to a neighborhood school, the dislocation can be overwhelming and devastating.

I believe very strongly that special education or treatment institutions should work diligently with the public school system in their area to set up an "aftercare" classroom, based on the caring classroom philosophy, as a transitional step for these students. The change in living arrangements, peer relationships, family relationships, in addition to the stress of coping with mainstreaming, can be dealt with more gently this way, supporting and consolidating what may still be very fragile gains. Gradually the students can increase their time in the regular classes and decrease their time in the aftercare class. The aftercare class can continue also to serve as a "time-out" area or crisis-intervention center for these students on an as-needed basis, as described above.

The teachers for the aftercare class can be trained in the institution's "caring classroom," which thus serves as a demonstration class, and then they in turn can serve as trainers for teachers in the public schools who are interested in developing techniques for affective learning in their own classes. Aftercare classes in the public schools, as well as in the institutions, can serve as assignments for student teachers or for graduate students doing advanced practicums. In this way, two needs can be addressed: the need for laboratory experience for graduate students and teacher trainees, and the need for transitional support for fragile students.

For such a recommendation to be implemented requires political savvy, and may be beyond the immediate interests, concerns or resources of the reader. For those of you who like to work toward systemic change, however, I offer it as food for thought. It is through such a project that the generalizing and strengthening of the caring the students have begun to learn in your classroom can be insured.

8. Prevention of Terminal

Burnout—Taking Care of Yourself

*U*p to this point the focus has been on giving care to others. But no caregiver can continue indefinitely without paying attention to caring for himself. If we don't take good care of ourselves, we will not long have anything to give others. We can, if we are careless of ourselves, "kill the goose that lays the golden egg." "Burnout" is the term for this phenomenon.

What It Is

Some people object to the word "burnout," saying that it is a fad, a popular notion which is a self-fulfilling prophesy: If you learn of it, you get it. I do not believe that.

I believe that most people can tolerate a lot of stress for limited periods of time and limited

amounts of stress for a long time, and that most people thrive on a modicum of stress as stimulating,
challenging to creativity, and energizing. However,
prolonged severe stress can and does take its toll
both physically and emotionally. Teaching children
with behavior disorders is a stressful occupation,*
and for the teacher who would stay in this profession it is important to have a plan for coping with
stress.

Burnout is the result of prolonged debilitating
stress, in which the balance between need satisfaction and frustration tips toward frustration too often
over too long a period of time. Burnout is a form of
depression. It can be either severe or incipient,
chronic or acute. If both chronic and severe, it can
result in the loss of the teacher to the profession, or
even in total breakdown and, in its severest state,
can lead to suicide.

Teachers of disturbed children are called on to
give regularly and consistently and indefinitely of
their emotional reserves. They give understanding,
knowledge, skills, caring—in ongoing relationships
on the job. When they go home, their family relationships require the same giving of the same resources. They are "paying out" all the time. If
anything tips the frustration-satisfaction balance,

---

*Indeed, it has been said that burnout among teachers
"threatens to reach hurricane force if it isn't checked soon." In
an essay in TIME (9/21/81) Lance Morrow wrote: "Burnout runs
through the teaching profession like Asian flue—possibly because it depresses people to be physically assaulted by those
they are trying to civilize."

either at school or at home, the result has ramifications in both places.

Satisfactions and replenishment must be forthcoming in one or both spheres, for the resources to meet the demands. When they aren't forthcoming, the stress builds, until it can result in burnout.

Symptoms of burnout are fatigue, irritability, anxiety, headache, appetite and sleep disturbances, loss of confidence, loss of feelings of self-worth, loss of goals or optimism about accomplishing them, boredom, and—in the final stages—anger, even rage, tearfulness, difficulty concentrating, impulsivity, loss of sleep, physical illness, loss of sexual desire; it can finally lead to quitting the job or doing something to get fired. Burnout is a legitimate occupational hazard, and it behooves us to prevent it when possible and treat it when it appears.

Prevention is the Best Approach

The following are things to consider in a plan to prevent burnout:

1. Have or develop skills, or have a consultant with skills, adequate to the task. If you are responsible for doing something that is significantly beyond your skills or knowledge, you can be subject to great stress, particularly if this situation exists over a long period. If you are just beginning to teach students with behavior disorders, find a mentor or a coach with whom

you can talk over ideas and problems, and from whom you can get suggestions. Reading this book and following the suggestions in it are a good first step. The methods presented here, particularly the use of the triads, are significantly stress-reducing. Having a coach or a peer support group or peer supervision is a very useful second step, giving you personal help on an ongoing basis.

2. Learn or practice skills for gaining support from your administrative system. When the system seems unresponsive to your needs, bring your political sophistication to bear on it. Negotiate. Trade off what you have that the system needs for what the system has that you need. (Examples of what you have that the system needs: Knowledge of how to obtain and retain state accreditation for your program; or a showplace for demonstrating how to work with difficult problem students; or protection from the marauding raids of aggressive students; or consultation on an IEP . . . etc. Examples of what the system has that you need: An aide, or a "holding area"; or a class of only one sex; or free periods interspersed with work periods; or a consultant; or an agreement that you be allowed to screen all students before accepting them; or that the administrator will support you in some specific way . . . etc.).

3. Examine your own personal needs and plan ahead for how you will satisfy them. (Examples: How much sleep do you require in order to feel good? Are you getting it? Or are you moonlight-

ing or otherwise encroaching on your sleep? If you cheat yourself of sleep too often too long, you are setting yourself up for debilitating stress. Do you eat a balanced diet, adequate for your needs? If you are overweight or not eating correctly, that can become a problem. Do you have a good balance of time for yourself and time spent with friends? Are you doing things for fun and relaxation that you look forward to, or is your life becoming one of drudgery and routine? You are a caregiver; do you have people who give care to you? Is their care sufficient and of good quality? If not, do something about that. Do you get enough physical exercise? Are you paying attention to your spiritual needs and growth? What about the way you are handling your finances—are you overspending your income and either taking on extra work or experiencing anxiety as a result? If so, ask yourself whether your lifestyle is worth the extra work and fatigue and anxiety. Consider the ultimate results of the fatigue and worry; should you make some different choices, e.g., adjust your expenses downward for better mental and physical health?)

If you have any concern about the questions referred to in the examples, make a plan for changing whatever aspect of your lifestyle seems to you to need change. Examine your values, what you want for yourself and how you can best fulfill your goals and needs. Do some classic problem-solving for yourself. The result will be a plan best calculated to prevent burnout. You will be in greater control, rather than at the mercy of random demands and frustrations.

Treatment, When Burnout Occurs

We all know the saying about the best-laid plans. Despite our thoughtful planning, and hopes for establishing a responsible lifestyle, we are not in control of all things at all times. Sometimes, despite our efforts, the system remains unresponsive, yet without our being ready to leave it; or unexpected problems arise in our private lives; or our workload is significantly increased; or our carefully-built support system folds on us; or we develop a debilitating illness; or suddenly all the students are going crazy at once and nothing we do seems to be working; or we have been doing the same things for too long without realizing we are overdue for a new challenge, a new opportunity to grow. Burnout can sneak up on us, silently and insidiously, and we may suddenly and with little warning find ourselves with a full-blown case of it.

Don't despair—take immediate steps to take care of yourself. As soon as you are aware that you are suffering from burnout (you know the symptoms, so you may be the first to recognize them in yourself; or your best friend, worst enemy, or administrator may tip you off), do as many as possible or necessary of the following:

1. Arrange to take a "mental health" day, in conjunction with the weekend, for at least the next two weeks. Sick leave should be taken for this. It is a legitimate use of sick leave.
2. Ask a colleague to take some of your duties, classes, or coverage responsibilities in exchange for your doing the same for him when he needs it.
3. Do *not* take tranquilizers! Avoid alcohol, caffeine, and sugar.*
4. Ask your administrator to help you change your schedule so you do not have two difficult classes back-to-back (sometimes possible if you do not have a self-contained classroom).
5. Practice stress-management tools such as The Summary Quieting Response—a deep-breathing exercist consisting of the following:

   a. Sit in a comfortable chair with your feet on the floor.
   b. Close your eyes and keep them closed.
   c. Smile gently to yourself and pull your shoulders back.
   d. Take two deep breaths, counting to 4 as you inhale and to 4 as you exhale. On the second breath, as you exhale, let your lips part, let your shoulders relax, and feel a wave of re-

---

*There is controversy over the role of sugar in stress. If your experience is that you tend to be more depressed or impulsive or irritable after eating sugar, it would be wise to avoid it at times of burnout.

211

laxation go through your whole body, from your head down to your feet.

e. Do a body scan, becoming aware of each part of your body, starting at the top of your head and proceeding to your feet; pay attention to such stress-reacting areas as forehead, teeth and jaw, back of neck, shoulders, abdominal muscles. Wherever you find tension, relax it.

f. Take several minutes to enjoy the feeling of relaxation you are experiencing.

Do this as many times a day as you think of it, but at least before meals and just before going to bed.

6. Talk with your coach and/or your peer support group about what is happening to you and get their help, suggestions, and "strokes." Ask for help and strokes; accept them.

7. Drop, temporarily or permanently, any non-essential boring and stress producing activities (such as committees that are taking more time and energy than they are worth).

8. If you are beginning to feel better after two weeks, you can gradually begin to resume your normal schedule. At this point, you may want to take on a new, interesting, energizing activity (such as learning a new skill), so long as it does not require too much time and energy and planning and dislocating. Plan some time-limited strictly-for-fun activities that you can do in the

next few days and look forward to in the near future.

9. Re-evaluate your prevention plan and make any adjustments indicated. This includes looking at your goals: Are any changes in order? How will you accomplish them?

10. Plan a restful vacation in which you will be doing things you enjoy but not wearing yourself out.

If you respect and care for yourself in these ways, you can treat your own burnout rather well and continue to go on giving care to others.

(A note to the administrator: Prevention and treatment of burnout is simply good management of your resources—your teaching staff. Support of the measures outlined above will pay off overwhelmingly in the long run, in greater staff satisfaction, efficiency, and higher standards of functioning. There will be less unplanned absence, and fewer casualties in the form of permanent loss to the profession.)

The Need for Supervision

Some educational models call for the teacher to be the source of knowledge—which is doled out to each student, who takes it and goes his individual way, earning his grade, often in competition with his peers for teacher time, attention, approval, reward. The teacher mainly needs mastery of his subject and how to test and grade it. Anything else is the student's problem.

Some models deal with discipline problems (such as the newly popular "Assertive Discipline"), giving clearcut rules and putting students on notice when they break the rules—it being ultimately the student's or principal's responsibility to find a way to correct the problem. Such models do not demand much in the way of supervision. A standard teacher-training course of study and a basic understanding of how to apply the rules and a little experience are all that are needed.

The Caring Classroom, however, makes more demands on the teacher to be a mature autonomous person. It is impossible to teach students non-violent alternatives to coping with frustration if one can only deal with frustrating students by paddling or punishing them. One must be non-violent himself to teach alternatives to violence. It is impossible to teach students responsible assertive ways to communicate if one is passive or indirect and manipulative in one's own communicating. It is impossible to teach students how to problem-solve if one is confused about problem-solving. It is impossible to teach students to care if one is distant or hostile.

Case Illustration Jeanne is an extremely intelligent woman who has taught home economics for a number of years, and has tenure. She knows a great deal about her field and has published a book. However, she has difficulty in her relationships with other people. She was divorced long ago and has never been able to form a close friendship with a man; she is distant from most of her family, but lends large amounts of money to her children and then worries about the thought that she won't ever get it back and may not have enough for her own needs.

She is warm and caring and giving toward peers and students at the expense of her own energy, often giving time and attention beyond what is needed or appropriate, after which she becomes angry and resentful of others for "not doing enough." She sets unrealistically high standards for herself and others, and is unforgiving when the standards aren't met. She alternates between love and hate, love and hate.

Jeanne has a high need for personal recognition, which she often gets because of her energy and talent. However, during the inevitable periods that come to us all when frustrations pile up and others seem to be ignoring or blind to how wonderful we are, Jeanne's symptoms of stress begin to overwhelm her: She becomes suspicious of her colleagues, angry, impulsive, and unable to create or innovate. Occasionally she has, in the past, impulsively changed jobs.

Jeanne chronically has difficulty problem-solving: At faculty meetings she often brings up a problem "which has no solution," and which brings the meeting to a confused stalemate, with the other members either looking puzzled or talking about a score of different things. (The reason for this is that her "problem" is really three or more separate problems disguised as one. If broken down into its separate parts, her "problem" then becomes solvable. In its original complex form, it is indeed incapable of being solved.) Frequently Jeanne does not want a solution, playing "yes, but . . ." in response to all her colleagues' suggestions, because she has a hidden agenda: her own hurt feelings, disguised as a practical difficulty with scheduling or work load.

Jeanne, therefore, has intelligence, expertise and experience in her specialty, tenure, energy, and is a caring, warm, giving person. However, if allowed to try to establish a Caring Classroom without close and expert supervision from a person who has the strengths that she lacks (stability of close caring relationships, clarity of communication, ability to set realistic limits on one's own expenditure of energy and caring, and skill at problem solving) the outcome would be disastrous. (Given her outstanding qualities, she might even end up being a supervisor herself, which would be an even worse disaster.)

If left to her own devices, Jeanne eventually recreates in her classroom the dependent loving-hating relationships characteristic of the rest of her life. She sets too high standards and punishes students who "let her down," putting them in confusing double-binds which neither she nor they understand. One of the most dangerous aspects of this is her lack of insight: Blind to her own problem, she has no idea why she is in pain so much of the time. Therefore she does not know what she needs help with, or how to ask for it. She needs close expert supervision—not in her field of expertise, but in the area of problem-solving and interpersonal relationships.

Supervision is a source of support, encouragement, clarification, information, coaching, correction, and strength. Few if any people have *all* the qualities desirable for teaching a caring classroom, but most schools will find all the qualities are present in the faculty collectively. Some faculty members will have certain qualities, and be able to use them to teach and supervise others. They, in turn, can get "coaching" in other qualities in which they need strengthening, from peers who are strong in those particular qualities. Thus, the strength can be shared, in much the same way the students help each other.

There are many styles of supervision, from the close "apprenticeship" with one supervisor, to group and peer supervision, to formal or informal "consultation." Flexibility is the goal, in determining which is the best form to meet the particular need. Maturity, tact, and the ability to support strengths and to confront weaknesses directly, compassionately, clearly, and in a business-like way are qualities needed for successful supervision or coaching.

School systems err seriously if they do not provide supervisory support both for newcomers to the profession and for experienced staff who are breaking ground in a new area. Teaching school has become increasingly demanding and hazardous. Forty years ago the main concerns of teachers were such things as truancy, gum-chewing, speaking out in class without permission, running in the corridors, unreturned library books, and failure to do homework. Teachers today are most concerned about violence and vandalism: guns and knives in school, assaults on teachers, assaults on students, wanton destruction of school property, and drugs and alcohol. One can be quickly overwhelmed by such concerns.

Conceivably you could take several years figuring out the best way to deal with gum-chewing, without significant loss of control of the educational process or serious less of self-esteem. No such luxury is possible in the case of learning to deal with violence or drug abuse. Even a single instance of violence may be one's last, and a succession of even "minor" incidents can do severe and long-lived damage to one's ability to teach, and one's feelings of confidence and self-worth.

If you are interested in building a Caring Classroom, and your administration has not provided you with supervision or consultation, ask for it. If it is still not forthcoming, the best favor you can do for yourself is to get an agreement with one or several of your colleagues for some informal "coaching," or find a professional person you respect outside the building or even outside the school system, who will be your coach or mentor.

Frequently your own peers will be a rich source of such help, and will be pleased and flattered by your request that they tutor you in their strong points. It is a test of your own maturity and security for you to be able to ask for help. (It is, however, only what you are asking the students to do in the Caring Classroom!) If there is nobody that you can find who does anything better than you, perhaps you can ask someone to help you develop humility and a more realistic insight.

You will be repaid many times over for such efforts in your own behalf.

> *Man belongs to man,*
> *Man has claims on Man.*

Albert Schweitzer

Suggested Readings

Bramhall, Martha Freis. "Burnout: The Subtle Thief of Program Effectiveness (Focus: Prevention)." Paper presented at the American Orthopsychiatric Association Annual Meeting, Toronto, Canada, April, 1980. (Mimeographed.)
A cookbook on burnout prevention.

Hoffer, Arthur. "A Mutual Support System For Helpers: Antidote for Professional Burnout." Paper read at the 57th Annual Meeting of the American Orthopsychiatric Association, Toronto, Canada, April, 1980. (Mimeographed.)

Reid, Kenneth. "Job Related Stress and the Mental Health Professional: the Emotional Cost Factor of the Helping Person." Paper presented at the 57th Annual Meeting of the American Orthopsychiatric Association, Toronto, Canada, April, 1980. (Mimeographed.)

Bibliography

Adler, Mortimer J. *The Paideia Proposal, An Educational Manifesto*. New York: MacMillan, 1982.

Aichhorn, August. *Wayward Youth*. New York: The Viking Press, 1935.

Alberti, R. E., and Emmons, M. L. *Your Perfect Right: A Guide to Assertive Behavior*. San Luis Obispo, California: Impact, 1974.

Alper, Michael. "All Our Children *Can* Learn." *University of Chicago Magazine*, Summer, 1982, Vol. 74, No. 4.

Bassin, Alexander, Bratter, Thomas E., and Rachin, Richard L. (eds.) *The Reality Therapy Reader*. New York: Harper and Row, 1976.

Berne, Eric, M.D. *Games People Play*. New York: Grove Press, 1964.

Bettelheim, Bruno. *Love Is Not Enough*. Glencoe, Ill.: The Free Press, 1950.

———. *Surviving, and Other Essays*. New York: Alfred A. Knopf, 1979.

———. Truants From Life, *The Rehabilitation of Emotionally Disturbed Children*. Glencoe, Ill.: The Free Press, 1955.

Bloom, Benjamin S. *All Our Children Learning, A Primer for Parents, Teachers, and Other Educators.* New York: McGraw-Hill, 1981.

Bowen, Murray, M.D. *Family Therapy in Clinical Practice.* New York: Jason Aronson, Inc., 1978.

Bower, S. A., and Bower, G. H. *Asserting Yourself, A Practical Guide for Positive Change.* Reading, Mass.: Addison-Wesley, 1976.

Bowlby, John. *Child Care And The Growth of Love.* (2nd Ed.). New York: Penguin Books, 1965.

Bramhall, Martha F. "Burnout: The Subtle Thief of Program Effectiveness (Focus: Prevention)." American Orthopsychiatric Association Annual Meeting, Toronto, Canada, 1980. (Mimeographed.)

Brandt, Anthony. "The Schools Where Everyone Gets A's," *Family Circle Magazine,* March 17, 1981.

Carducci, Dewey J. "Positive Peer Culture and Assertiveness Training: Complementary Modalities for Dealing With Disturbed and Disturbing Adolescents in the Classroom," *Behavioral Disorders,* May, 1980.

———. "They're Asking For It," *The American Teacher,* American Federation of Teachers, Feb., 1972.

Cheek, Donald K., Ph.D. *Assertive Black . . . Puzzled White*. San Luis Obispo, Calif.: Impact, 1976.

Comer, James P. *School Power*. New York: The Free Press, 1980.

Cousins, Norman. *Anatomy of an Illness*. New York: W. W. Norton, 1979.

————. *Human Options*. New York: W. W. Norton, 1981.

Dennison, George. *The Lives of Children*. New York: Random House, 1969.

Diagnostic and Statistical Manual of Mental Disorders (Third Edition). Washington, D.C.: The American Psychiatric Association, 1980.

Erikson, Erik. *Childhood and Society*. New York: W. W. Norton, 1950.

Erikson, Robert, and Carducci, Judith. "Assertiveness Training Interventions and the Alcoholic Family System," National Council on Alcoholism Annual Forum, Washington, D.C., April, 1979. (Xeroxed.)

Fader, Daniel. *The New Hooked on Books*. New York: Berkley Publishing Co., 1976.

Fantini, Mario. "Disciplined Caring," *The Phi Delta Kappan,* Nov., 1980.

Fraiberg, Selma. *The Magic Years.* New York: Charles Scribners' Sons, 1959.

Freud, Anna. *The Ego and the Mechanisms of Defense.* New York: International Universities Press, Inc., 1946.

Gartner, Alan, Kohler, Mary, and Riessman, Frank. *Children Teach Children, Learning by Teaching.* New York: Harper and Row, 1971.

Glasser, William, M.D. *Positive Addiction.* New York: Harper and Row, 1976.

————. *Reality Therapy.* New York: Harper and Row, 1965.

Goldstein, Arnold P., Sprafkin, Robert P., Gershaw, N. Jane, and Klein, Paul. *Skillstreaming the Adolescent, A Structured Learning Approach to Teaching Prosocial Skills.* Champaign, Ill.: Research Press, 1980.

Guerin, Philip J., Jr., M.D. (ed.). *Family Therapy, Theory and Practice.* New York: Gardner Press, 1976.

Harris, Thomas A., M.D. *I'm OK—You're OK.* New York: Harper and Row, 1969.

Harshman, Hardwick W. (ed.). *Educating the Emotionally Disturbed, A Book of Readings*. New York: Thomas Y. Crowell, 1969.

Hoffer, Arthur. "A Mutual Support System For Helpers: Antidote for Professional Burnout." American Orthopsychiatric Association Annual Meeting, Toronto, Canada, 1980. (Mimeographed.)

Jakubowski, P., and Lange, A. J. *The Assertive Option, Your Rights and Responsibilities*. Champaign, Ill.: Research Press, 1978.

James, Muriel, and Jongeward, Dorothy. *Born to Win*. Reading, MA: Addison-Wesley, 1971.

Lange, A. J., and Jakubowski, P. *Responsible Assertive Behavior, Cognitive/Behavioral Procedures for Trainers*. Champaign, Ill.: Research Press, 1976.

Long, Nicholas, Morse, William C., and Newman, Ruth G. (eds.). *Conflict in the Classroom: The Education of Emotionally Disturbed Children*. Belmont, Calif.: Wadsworth Publishing Co., 1965.

Montagu, M. F. Ashley. *The Direction of Human Development*. New York: Harper and Brothers, 1955.

Morrow, Lance. "Burnout." *TIME,* Sept., 1981.

Morse, William C., et. al. *Affective Education for Special Children and Youth*. Reston, Va.: The Council for Exceptional Children, 1980.

———. *Classroom Disturbance: The Principal's Dilemma*. Arlington, Va.: The Council for Exceptional Children, 1971.

Pearson, Craig. *Resolving Classroom Conflict*. Palo Alto, Calif.: Learning Handbooks, 1974.

Redl, Fritz. *When We Deal With Children*. New York: The Free Press, 1966.

———. and Wineman, David. *Children Who Hate, The Disorganization and Breakdown of Behavior Controls*. New York: The Free Press, 1951.

———. *Controls From Within, Techniques for the Treatment of the Aggressive Child*. New York: The Free Press, 1952.

Reid, Kenneth, Ph.D. "Job Related Stress and the Mental Health Professional: The Emotional Cost Factor of the Helping Person," American Orthopsychiatric Association Annual Meeting, Toronto, Canada, April, 1980. (Mimeographed.)

Rothman, Esther P. *Troubled Teachers*. New York: David McKay, 1977.

Smith, Lendon, M.D. *Improving Your Child's Behavior Chemistry*. Englewood Cliffs, N.J.: Prentice-Hall, 1976.

Smith, Manuel, Ph.D. *When I Say No I Feel Guilty*. New York: The Dial Press, 1975.

Strain, Phillip S. (ed.). *The Utilization of Classroom Peers as Behavior Change Agents*. New York: Plenum Press, 1981.

Trieschman, Albert E., et. al. *The Other 23 Hours*. Chicago: Aldine Publishing Co., 1969.

Tutt, Norman. *Care or Custody*. New York: Agathon Press, 1975.

Vogel, Jerome, M.D. *A Stress Test for Children—Is Your "Problem Child's" Problem Nutrition? Here's How to Find Out*. New Canaan, Conn.: Keats Publishing Co., 1983.

Vorrath, Harry, and Brendtro, Larry K. *Positive Peer Culture*. Chicago: Aldine Publishing Co., 1974.

Wheelis, Allen. *How People Change*. New York: Harper and Row, 1970.

Wiener, Harvey. *Any Child Can Write*. New York: McGraw-Hill, 1978.

Yalom, Irvin D., M.D. *The Theory and Practice of Group Psychotherapy*. New York: Basic Books, 1975.